Test Best® for Success

LEVEL
C

STECK-VAUGHN

A Harcourt Company

www.steck-vaughn.com

ACKNOWLEDGMENTS

Contributing Authors

Richard Crowe
Dan Dramer
Alvin Kravitz, Ed.D.
Marlene S. Roth, M.S.
Marren L. Simmons, M.S.

Illustrations

Debbie Dieneman
Jack Kershner/Lancelot Art Studio
Scott Trerrotola

Photo Credits

p.32 ©Mike Powell/Allsport/Getty Images; pp.34, 69 ©AP/Wide World Photos; p.70 ©Doug Bensinger/Allsport/Getty Images; p.76 ©AP/Wide World Photos.

Steck-Vaughn is indebted to the following for permission to use material in this book:

page 10 *Big Sister and Little Sister* by Charlotte Zolotow. Text copyright © 1966 by Charlotte Zolotow; text copyright © renewed 1994 by Charlotte Zolotow. Used by permission of HarperCollins Publishers.

page 12 "Comfortable Old Chair" from *Dogs and Dragons, Trees and Dreams* by Karla Kuskin. Copyright © 1980. Reprinted by permission of the author.

page 55 "The Green Chicken" from *Stories to Tell a Cat* by Alvin Schwartz. Copyright © 1992 by Alvin Schwartz. Used by permission of HarperCollins Publishers.

ISBN 0-7398-6728-8

Copyright ©2003 Steck-Vaughn Company

2 3 4 5 6 7 8 9   08 07 06 05 04 03

Test Best® for Success Level C

Table of Contents

TO THE TEACHER

Test Best for Success is an instructional series for you to use with your students. As teachers, you know that children learn best by doing. Therefore, we have developed a series that will actively involve your students while they learn and apply specific strategies in answering questions about what they have read. Specific learning strategies will be presented through modeling and practice. Varying degrees of support, structure, and explanation are provided.

Many genres, such as fiction, nonfiction, poems, fables, and folk tales are included. Some of the passages are taken from published, authentic literature reflecting the type of instruction that exists in classrooms today. The questions following each passage reflect different levels of comprehension. The material in this book provides your students with step-by-step instruction that will maximize their reading success in classroom work as well as in testing situations.

Test Taking Strategies

Three specific strategies, which are designed to assist the students in answering questions, are presented here.

Modeled Instruction

Instruction and practice are provided for specific assessment objectives.

Test Practice

Students have the opportunity to practice all the strategies that they have learned. This section can be used to simulate tests. It may be used to evaluate students' progress and to assess further needs.

Reading Comprehension: Test-Taking Strategies

Section I:

Three Levels of Comprehension
There are three levels of comprehension.

Level 1: Basic Understanding
This is called the literal level of comprehension. It is also called recalling information. **The facts you need to know are written in the story.** If you look at the story you will see the information that you need.

Level 2: Analyzing information
This is called the interpretive level of comprehension. It is also called constructing meaning. **This is using the information that you read in the story and figuring out what it means.** You use the facts you read and decide how they go together. This level also involves analyzing form. This is when you analyze the parts that make up a story or the story type.

Level 3: Evaluating and Extending information
This is called the critical level of comprehension. It is also called extending and evaluating meaning. **This is thinking about the story and adding what you know from your own experiences.** You may also think about what the author meant.

Section II:

The Three Strategies
There are three strategies you can use to help you answer questions.

STRATEGY 1
The CHECK AND SEE Strategy
The **Check and See Strategy** can be used when a question asks you to remember a fact from the story. The answer to the question is right there in the passage. It is not hidden. Some of the same words may be in the story and in the question.

 Check and See will help you answer *remembering information* questions.

This is the **Check and See Strategy**

1. READ: *Read the question.*

2. FIND: *Find the information you need in the passage.*

3. DECIDE: **Decide** *which strategy to use:*
    Check and See: *Put a* **check** *next to the sentence where you can* **see** *the words you need to answer the question.*

4. ANSWER: *Choose the best* **answer.**

GUIDED INSTRUCTION: Here is a story with a question using the **Check and See Strategy**. *You do this one.*

When students search for an answer to a science problem, they use the scientific method. They learn to state the problem and gather information. After that, they form a hypothesis, which is a guess as to the solution to the problem. Next, an experiment is done and information is recorded and analyzed. Finally, a conclusion is reached. The scientific method is a procedure that students will use over and over again. It is an orderly and systematic way to solve a problem.

What is the scientific method?

A. a guess to solve a problem
B. an orderly and systematic way to solve a problem
C. a very important science experiment
D. information that is recorded and analyzed

Using the Check and See Strategy:

1. **READ:** *Read the question.*

2. **FIND:** *Find the information you need in the passage.*

3. **DECIDE:** *Decide which strategy to use.*
   Check and See: *Put a check next to the sentence in the passage.*

4. **ANSWER:** *Choose the best answer.*

The best answer is _____.

STRATEGY 2

The PUZZLE PIECE Strategy

The **Puzzle Piece Strategy** is another strategy you can use. Sometimes you may be asked a question that does not seem to have an answer. The answer is not right there in the story for you to see.

 Puzzle Piece is a strategy you can use when you must fit pieces of information together to get the answer. This is like putting a puzzle together. Puzzles are made up of several pieces. You cannot look at one piece and know what the picture is. Only when you put the puzzle pieces together can you see the whole picture.

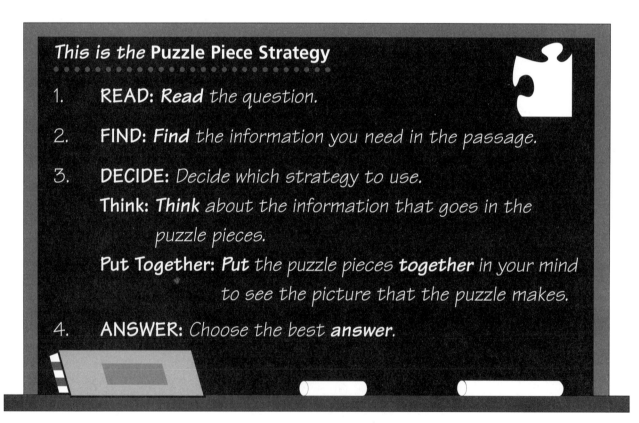

This is the Puzzle Piece Strategy

1. **READ:** *Read* the question.

2. **FIND:** *Find* the information you need in the passage.

3. **DECIDE:** *Decide which strategy to use.*

   Think: *Think* about the information that goes in the puzzle pieces.

   Put Together: *Put* the puzzle pieces **together** in your mind to see the picture that the puzzle makes.

4. **ANSWER:** *Choose the best* **answer**.

Constructing Meaning

Use the **Puzzle Piece Strategy** to answer questions that ask about the main idea, the best title for a story, or what the story is mostly about. It can also be used to answer questions that ask about what might happen next or what the author's purpose is. These kinds of questions are called *constructing meaning* questions.

 MODELED INSTRUCTION: Here is a story for you to read. See how the **Puzzle Piece Strategy** *is used.*

Many of the types of food we eat in our school cafeteria originated in other countries. The most popular lunch is pizza, which originally came from Italy. A Mexican favorite of many of our students is tacos. They are easy to make and fun to eat. A new addition in our cafeteria is egg rolls. These came from China. Another favorite is frankfurters. Many people think that franks are an American food. That is not true. Where do you think they came from?

 What is the best title for this selection?

    A.   "All American Foods"
    B.   "Friday Is Pizza Day"
    C.   "International Lunches"
    D.   "Mexican Favorites"

 Using the **Puzzle Piece Strategy**

1.   **READ:** *Read the question.*

2.   **FIND:** *Find the information you need.*

3.   **DECIDE:** *Decide which strategy to use.*

4.   **ANSWER:** *Choose the best answer.* Foods from many countries are found in the cafeteria.
The best answer is *C: "International Lunches"*

Analyzing Form

You can also use the **Puzzle Piece Strategy** to answer questions that ask about the parts that make up a story. The parts of a story are the *characters, setting, plot,* and *mood.*

Characters
- the people, animals, or things the story is about

Setting
- where and when the story takes place

Plot
- all the events that happen in the story

Mood
- the main feeling in the story

The **Puzzle Piece Strategy** is a strategy you can also use to answer questions that ask about what kind of story you have read. *Is it a fable, mystery, biography, or other type?*

Questions about how stories are put together or their type are called *analyzing form* questions. The **Puzzle Piece Strategy** can be used to answer all of these questions.

*GUIDED INSTRUCTION: Here is another story for you to read with a question needing the **Puzzle Piece Strategy**. Do this one on your own.*

This year in school I learned about the history of New England, a part of the United States. Most of what I learned I read from books and listening to my teacher. My family decided to take a vacation during the summer. Mom and Dad wanted to go to New England. They thought it would be a stimulating place to go on vacation. They thought I would enjoy seeing some of the places I learned about in school. I could not get that enthusiastic about seeing the educational sights of New England. I wasn't sure if this was the place where I wanted to go on vacation. New England didn't seem all that great to me. I thought the trip would be dull and boring.

How does the writer feel about the trip?
A. excited and anxious
B. concerned but hopeful
C. eager and ungrateful
D. unenthusiastic and doubtful

*Using the **Puzzle Piece Strategy***

1. **READ:** *Read the question.*

2. **FIND:** *Find the information you need in the passage.*

Hint: Questions about how a person feels in a story are asking about the mood.

3. **DECIDE:** *Decide which strategy to use.*

4. **ANSWER:** *Choose the best answer.*

The best answer is _____.

Strategy 3

The WHAT LIGHTS UP Strategy

What Lights Up is another strategy you can use when the answer is not right there. This time you add information from your own experiences.

What Lights Up can help you decide if something is important, true, real, useful, or a fact in the story. It can help you decide what would happen if the story went on or the ending was different.

You can use the **What Lights Up Strategy** to help you answer the hardest type of question. This is when you are asked to read and think beyond what is written. These questions are called *extending and evaluating meaning* questions.

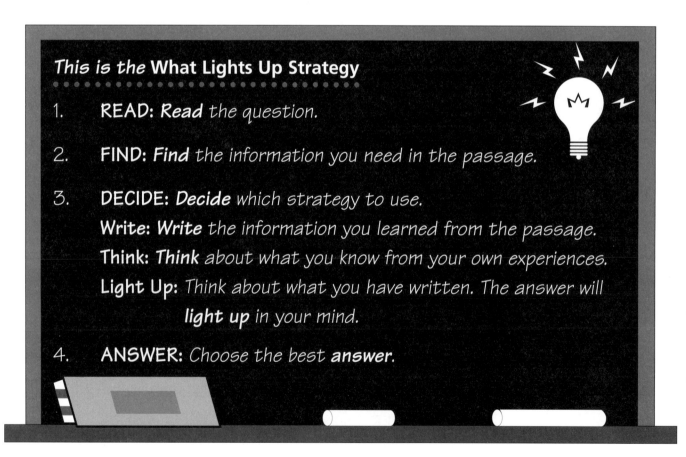

This is the What Lights Up Strategy

1. READ: *Read* the question.

2. FIND: *Find* the information you need in the passage.

3. DECIDE: *Decide* which strategy to use.

    Write: *Write* the information you learned from the passage.

    Think: *Think* about what you know from your own experiences.

    Light Up: Think about what you have written. The answer will **light up** in your mind.

4. ANSWER: *Choose* the best **answer**.

Do you know Aesop's fable about the fox and the grapes? One hot summer's day a fox was walking in the woods. He was very tired and very hungry but most of all he was thirsty. He suddenly saw a bunch of fat, juicy purple grapes hanging from a vine high above his head. He tried to reach the grapes but could not. He stepped back and took a running jump, but failed again. Finally, he stopped trying. As he walked away he said, "Who wants those grapes, anyway? They are probably sour."

 With which sentence would the fox probably agree?

    A.   Slow and steady wins the race.

    B.   Do not try for grapes that are hard to reach.

    C.   If you do not succeed, try again.

    D.   What is hard to obtain is worthless.

Using the **What Lights Up Strategy**

1.   **READ:** Read the question.

2.   **FIND:** Find the information you need in the passage.

3.   **DECIDE:** Decide which strategy to use.
Write: Write the information you learned from the passage.
Think: Think about what you know from your own experiences. Write that information.
Light Up: Think about what you have written. The answer will light up in your mind.

4.   **ANSWER:** Choose the best answer.

The best answer is _____.

Reading Comprehension

Objectives

Objective 1: Basic Understanding

Demonstrate understanding of the literal meaning of a passage through identifying stated information, indicating sequence of events, and defining vocabulary.

Objective 2: Analyze Text

Demonstrate comprehension by drawing conclusions; inferring relationships such as cause and effect; and identifying theme and story elements such as plot, climax, character, and setting.

Objective 3: Evaluate and Extend Meaning

Demonstrate critical understanding by making predictions; distinguishing between fact and opinion, and reality and fantasy; transferring ideas to other situations; and judging author purpose, point of view, and effectiveness.

Objective 4: Identify Reading Strategies

Demonstrate awareness of techniques that enhance comprehension, such as using existing knowledge, summarizing content, comparing information across texts, using graphics and text structure, and formulating questions that deepen understanding.

Objective 1: Defining Vocabulary

Sometimes you can figure out the meaning of a new word by using the words around it as clues.

Sherlock Holmes is a great detective. But he lives only in books. The <u>tales</u> about him have been written in 57 languages.

1   **In this paragraph, the word <u>tales</u> means —**

   ◯   places.

   ◯   names.

   ◯   stories.

   ◯   pens.

Hint: You get a clue as to what the word <u>tales</u> means by reading sentences 2 and 3.

Marie did not know how to operate the compact disc player. She read the <u>manual</u>. She hoped she could find the information she needed in the book.

2   **In this paragraph, the word <u>manual</u> means —**

   ◯   a dictionary.

   ◯   a compact disc.

   ◯   a recipe book.

   ◯   a how-to book.

Hint: You get a clue as to what the word <u>manual</u> means from the sentence after the one in which the word appears.

Mother ducks often take their <u>ducklings</u> swimming. When a pond is full of mothers and babies, the mother ducks quack and swim around. Whichever mother duck quacks the loudest gets the greatest number of <u>ducklings</u> to swim around her.

3   **In this paragraph, the word <u>ducklings</u> means —**

   ◯   mother ducks

   ◯   baby ducks

   ◯   loud ducks

   ◯   quacking ducks

Hint: You get a clue as to what the word <u>ducklings</u> means from the second sentence in the paragraph.

Pat grew up wanting to be a postmaster. As a boy, whenever he went to the post office in his home town in Ohio, he would dream of running it. When he finished school, his dream almost came true. He became a postmaster, but in a different town in Ohio.

4 In this paragraph, the word postmaster means —

○ someone who likes to collect stamps.

○ an expert about postage.

○ a person in charge of a post office.

○ the person who posts time for runners.

Hint: You get a clue as to what the word postmaster means from the sentence that tells about Pat's dream.

Birds perch on a tree even while they sleep. Their toes grab the branch so they don't fall. Three toes point forward. One toe points backward. The toes lock tightly onto the branch.

5 In this paragraph, the word perch means —

○ fly.

○ sit.

○ vanish.

○ promise.

Hint: You get a clue as to what the word perch means by reading the sentences after the one in which the word is.

Doctors studied thousands of people. Some of the people spent a lot of time alone. Many of these people had weak hearts. They were more likely to have a heart attack. Other people spent a lot of time with their families and friends. Most of these social people had strong hearts.

6 In this paragraph, someone who is social —

○ spends time with people

○ goes to the doctor's office

○ studies people's health

○ has a weak heart

Hint: You get a clue as to what the word social means by reading the sentence before the word.

Facts or details are important. By noticing them, you will know what the passage is about.

The United States Supreme Court is the highest court of the land. For many years, only men were Supreme Court judges. That was true until 1981. That year, Sandra Day O'Connor became a Supreme Court judge. She was the first woman to do so.

Sandra's first teacher was her mother. Later, Sandra went to school. Sandra finished high school when she was just 16. Then, she followed her dream to study law. She was in law school for five years. When she finished law school, she couldn't find a job. Very few companies wanted women lawyers!

7   Only men served on the Supreme Court —

    ◯ after 1990.

    ◯ after 1811.

    ◯ until 1981.

    ◯ until 200 years ago.

Hint: Look at sentences 2 and 3.

8   The highest court of the United States is the —

    ◯ World Court.

    ◯ State Court.

    ◯ Supreme Court.

    ◯ Day Court.

Hint: Look for this sentence in the passage.

9   What was Sandra's dream?

    ◯ to finish high school

    ◯ to find a job

    ◯ to study law

    ◯ to be a teacher

Hint: Look at sentence 9.

Sandra married a man she met in law school. They both got jobs as lawyers. For a while, Sandra had her own law office. Then, she and her husband had a son. Sandra decided to stay home. Sandra and her husband had two more sons.

After nine years, Sandra became a judge in Arizona. She was a judge there for seven years. Then, one of the judges from the Supreme Court left. So the Supreme Court needed another judge. The President of the United States heard about Sandra. He asked her to become a judge on the Supreme Court. She eagerly said, "Yes!"

10 **The President asked Sandra Day O'Connor to be a —**

○ student at a university.

○ lawyer in Arizona.

○ judge in an Arizona court.

○ judge on the Supreme Court.

Hint: Find the section that talks about the President.

11 **Sandra had —**

○ three sons.

○ two daughters.

○ a son and a daughter.

○ four children.

Hint: Count the number of sons mentioned in the passage.

12 **Sandra and her husband were both —**

○ doctors.

○ lawyers.

○ teachers.

○ bankers.

Hint: Look at sentence 2.

13 **How long was Sandra a judge in her state?**

○ two years

○ seven years

○ nine years

○ sixteen years

Hint: Look at sentence 7.

It is helpful to put events in the order they happened. This may help you to understand a passage.

Long, long ago, the ancient Greeks served a god named Zeus. They honored Zeus by giving grand festivals. The festivals were held in a place called Olympia. During the festivals, athletes showed their strength and speed. These festivals were the first Olympic Games.

In the year 776 B.C., the 200-meter race was won by a young man named Coroebus. He is the first Olympic winner on record. The next festival took place in 772 B.C. This time the Greeks wanted to offer more to their god. So, they held new sporting events. Many people came to watch them. For the next 1,000 years, the Olympics were held every four years. They always took place in Olympia.

At first, only people with money could afford to be Olympic athletes. They had the time to train and get in shape. Some of the events were horse racing, wrestling, boxing, and running. The first Olympics lasted for five days. Prizes were given on the last day. Winning was the most important part of athletics for the ancient Greeks. The winners marched in a parade toward the Temple of Zeus. Along the way, crowds tossed flowers at them. The winners wore olive wreaths. The Greeks gave prizes to the first-place winners only. People teased the losers.

The games were stopped in A.D. 393. At that time, the Romans ruled Greece. The emperor did not like the Greek gods. So, he stopped the Olympic events. The Greek temples stood empty. Over the years, they were buried by floods and earthquakes. In 1892, a Frenchman wanted to start the Olympic Games once again. He thought that the games would bring the people of the world together in peace. In 1896, he succeeded. The first modern games were held in Athens, Greece.

14 **When did the Olympic festivals stop?**

○ when they ran out of prizes

○ when the temples were flooded

○ 776 B.C.

○ A.D. 393

Hint: Look at the last paragraph.

15 **When were prizes given?**

○ on the first day

○ after each event

○ on the fifth day

○ every day

Hint: Look at the section mentioning the prizes.

16 **Which of these events happened last in the story?**

○ Coroebus won a race in Olympia.

○ A Frenchman wanted to start the Olympic Games once again.

○ Games were held in Athens, Greece.

○ Prizes were only given to first-place winners.

Hint: Look at the last paragraph.

17 **Which of these happened first in the story?**

○ The Greeks held a festival in 772 B.C.

○ The Roman emperor stopped the games in Olympia.

○ The Greeks held a festival in 776 B.C.

○ Some events were horse racing, wrestling, boxing, and running.

Hint: Look at the beginning of the story.

18 **When were the first modern Olympic games held?**

○ 772 B.C.

○ 200 B.C.

○ 1892

○ 1896

Hint: Look at the section about the modern Olympics.

Objective 2: Drawing Conclusions

The way a character acts tells you about that person's mood.

Al had been standing in line at the counter waiting to pay for the things he had chosen. The store was hot, and the air conditioning didn't work. Al was holding some heavy objects, and he wished the line would move faster. A woman cut to the front of the line. People protested, but the woman didn't budge. Suddenly, Al threw his things into a nearby cart and walked quickly out of the store.

1   How was Al feeling when he left the store?

○   Al had gotten tired of waiting and planned to come back when the store wasn't so busy.

○   Al was hungry and looking forward to lunch.

○   Al was angry that he had waited so long only to have someone cut into the line.

○   Al felt that he had chosen the wrong items.

Hint: Carefully think about the entire passage, especially the last sentence.

Ian and Louise were supposed to be planting corn, beans, and carrots together. While Louise dug up the old garden and turned over the soil, Ian sat under a tree sipping a cool drink. While Louise dug in fertilizer and raked the garden, Ian ate his lunch. When the soil was finally ready for the seeds to be planted, Ian said to Louise, "I'll plant the seeds." Louise yelled back, "No, thanks! I'll plant the seeds!"

2   How did Louise feel?

○   disgusted

○   alarmed

○   curious

○   grateful

Hint: You must read the entire passage and what Louise said at the end of the story to find out how Louise felt.

When the baby came home from the hospital, his five-year-old brother, Mike, shouted, "Take it back! You got a new baby because I'm not good enough for you!" Mike's parents talked with him for a long time. They told him that the baby would need special care at first. But that didn't mean they didn't love Mike anymore.

3 How did Mike feel about his new baby brother?

○ Mike was mad because the baby cried all the time.

○ Mike was mad because he didn't want to take care of the baby.

○ Mike felt his parents loved the new baby more than they loved him.

○ Mike felt that the baby should not get special care.

Hint: Read what Mike said to discover how he felt.

A fisherman brought a large fish to the king and was paid well for it. As the fisherman left, he picked up a valuable coin from the floor. The angry king called to him, "That is not yours." The man answered, "I did not want someone to step on the king's face. That is why I picked up the coin." The king smiled and let the man keep the coin.

4 How did the king feel after the man said something?

○ greedy

○ understood

○ upset

○ respected

Hint: Carefully think about the entire passage, especially what the king did at the end of the passage.

The setting of a story lets you know when and where the story is taking place.

Richard Byrd stood outside the small cabin on March 28, 1934. He shook hands with the men who were leaving. They were heading back to the main camp on the east coast of Antarctica. He would stay at the base camp for the winter. There was plenty of food and fuel in the tiny cabin. He felt sure nothing would go wrong.

But something did go wrong. Byrd was burning kerosene for heat, and the fumes were poisoning him. He continued to make his radio messages, because he didn't want anyone to try to rescue him in the dangerous weather. Byrd managed to stay alive until August, when three men arrived at the base camp. They hardly recognized Byrd. He was very thin and looked terrible. Byrd greeted them and then fell to the ground. The men had arrived in the nick of time. After two months of care, Byrd's good health returned.

5   **The story takes place —**

   ◯   100 years ago.

   ◯   within the past 25 years.

   ◯   over 60 years ago.

   ◯   in 1943.

   Hint: Read the first sentence.

6   **The story takes place —**

   ◯   at the main camp.

   ◯   on the coast of Antarctica.

   ◯   in a large cabin.

   ◯   at the base camp.

   Hint: Read the first paragraph.

7   **When was Richard Byrd rescued?**

   ◯   after two months of trouble

   ◯   while listening to messages

   ◯   in dangerous weather

   ◯   in August

   Hint: Find the section that talks about Byrd's rescue.

The strongest earthquake in the United States happened in Missouri. It took place in 1811. The center of the earthquake was near a town called New Madrid. Since few people lived near this town, nobody was killed. But the earthquake was quite strong. It changed the course of the Mississippi River.

8 When did the earthquake occur?

○ in 1911

○ in 1918

○ in 1811

○ in 1981

Hint: Look at the second sentence.

9 Where was the center of the earthquake?

○ near New Madrid

○ outside Missouri

○ along the Mississippi River

○ in a large town in Missouri

Hint: Read the first three sentences.

Going to the horse show on that beautiful summer day was a great experience. Before the events started, we were able to get very close to the riders and their horses. Then, after we found our seats, we spent the afternoon watching each rider and horse perform. At the end of the day, the best performers were given ribbons and prizes.

10 When is this story taking place?

○ in the summer

○ in the spring

○ at night

○ in the morning

Hint: Look at the first sentence.

Objective 2: Inferring Relationships

Knowing what happened (effect) and what made it happen (cause) helps you to understand what you read.

The big dance was Friday night, and Jodi needed a dress to wear. As she was sorting through her closet, her older sister, Gabriela, tapped her on the shoulder. She knew that Jodi had always liked her blue dress. "How would you like to wear this?" she asked. Jodi's eyes lit up. She hugged Gabriela and ran to try on the dress.

11   Why was Jodi happy?

○   Gabriela hugged Jodi.

○   Her sister got Jodi's attention.

○   Jodie could wear Gabriela's blue dress.

○   Jodi was trying to find a special dress.

Hint: Jodi's eyes lighting up is the effect. What made this happen?

12   Why did Jodi need a dress to wear?

○   She wanted to be like her older sister, Gabriela.

○   The big dance was Friday night.

○   She was tired of blue dresses in her closet.

○   She couldn't find any dresses in her closet.

Hint: Jodi needing a dress is the effect. What made this happen?

Alex and Vince were spending a week at camp. Tonight was their last night, and it was "skit night." The campers in each cabin had written plays about their camp experiences. Alex had seen how easily Vince made friends with everyone in the camp. When Vince was chosen to be the announcer for skit night, Alex dumped a box of cookie crumbs in Vince's sleeping bag.

13 Why did the campers write plays about their camp experiences?

   ○ They liked to write plays.

   ○ They had so much fun at camp that they had a lot to write about.

   ○ They were going to put on skits.

   ○ Their camp counselors asked them to write plays.

Hint: Writing plays is the effect. What made this happen?

14 Why did Alex dump a box of cookie crumbs in Vince's sleeping bag?

   ○ Vince was chosen to be the announcer for skit night.

   ○ Alex knew how much his friend liked cookies.

   ○ Alex wanted to have a party in the cabin after skit night.

   ○ Vince needed more cookies because he had so many friends.

Hint: Alex dumping a box of cookies in Vince's sleeping bag is the effect. What made this happen?

15 Why was Vince chosen as the announcer for skit night?

   ○ It was the last night of camp.

   ○ Vince was going home.

   ○ Vince made many friends.

   ○ He had written a play.

Hint: Being chosen as announcer is the effect. What made this happen?

Trena's baseball team was not very good. It had not won a game all season. Something had to be done, or else the team would be laughed at by everyone in town. So, Trena promised to eat one bug for every run the team scored. That night, the team scored twenty runs and finally won a game.

16 Why hadn't Trena's baseball team won a game all season?

   ○ Everyone in town laughed at the team.

   ○ The team ate bugs and got sick.

   ○ The team was not very good.

   ○ Something interrupted practices.

Hint: Not winning a game is the effect. What made this happen?

17 Why did the team score twenty runs?

   ○ They ate bugs before the game.

   ○ They had many fans in town.

   ○ There were twenty girls on the team.

   ○ Trena had promised to eat one bug for every run scored.

Hint: Scoring twenty runs is the effect. What made this happen?

Objective 3: Making Predictions

Many times you can tell in advance what is probably going to happen next. You must think about what would make sense if the story were to go on.

In the morning, Becky came downstairs. "I don't like this house at all," the girl told her parents. "It smells funny." Her mother asked if she had seen the wild strawberries growing in the front yard. Her father mentioned the pony he had seen at the neighboring house. The girl's eyes lit up.

1   What will Becky probably do?

○ The family will sell the house and move because of the smell.

○ The father will buy the pony for Becky.

○ Becky will find some things she likes about that house.

○ Becky will get angry because her eyes have lit up.

Hint: Think about how Becky feels at the end of the story, before you make your choice.

The man was trying to balance himself. His bicycle was picking up speed on the steep hill. He hit a bump, and one foot lost its grip on the pedal.

2   What will probably happen next?

○ The man will go down the hill faster.

○ The man will put his foot back on the pedal.

○ The bicycle will fall apart.

○ The man will fall off his bicycle.

Hint: Picture the scene in your mind before writing the answer.

The shaggy animal went up to the back door. It rattled the screen door with its front paw and then sat down. It was quiet for a while. But soon a face appeared at the door, and then there was a scream of joy. "It's Goldie!" a girl's voice said. "She's come back."

3   What will the girl probably do next?

○ run to get her mother

○ open the door to let Goldie in

○ shut and lock the inside door

○ scream again

Hint: What is most likely to happen next?

Valentina Tereshkova was nervous. She knew she'd soon make history. It was a still morning. She sat strapped in her seat. At last, the Soviet spaceship began to shake. Its great engines roared. The ship climbed from the launch pad. It built up speed. Soon, it was racing through the sky. Valentina had become the first woman in space.

4   What will Valentina probably do next?

○   call her mother

○   have lunch

○   follow the steps she was trained to do in space

○   rest so that she could think clearly

Hint: What seems most likely to happen based on all the sentences?

Cris looked at the window to make sure it was open. Then she marked her place and closed the book. She put it on the table next to her bed. Then she fluffed up the pillow and set the alarm clock.

5   What will Cris most likely do next?

○   fall asleep

○   have a snack

○   get into bed

○   take a shower

Hint: Read the entire paragraph.

When Sammy woke up, he looked out the window. The slopes were covered with snow. Quickly, he pulled on his long underwear and other warm clothes. He ate a good, hot breakfast so that he'd have plenty of energy. Then he checked his equipment. He walked in his heavy boots toward the door.

6   What is probably going to happen next?

○   Sammy is going to ski down the slopes.

○   Sammy is going ice skating.

○   Sammy is going to play golf.

○   Sammy is going to stay inside.

Hint: You need to read the whole paragraph, but especially the last sentence.

Objective 3: Distinguishing Between Fact and Opinion

It is important to know the difference between fact and opinion. A fact is real and true. An opinion is a feeling or belief. Words that describe are used to offer opinions.

Stephen Hawking is a famous scientist. He has written books about physics and our universe. But Hawking must do all his work in a wheelchair. In his twenties, he found out that he had Lou Gehrig's disease. Later, he lost his power to speak and write. Now, he does all his work on a special computer. The computer allows him to speak.

7   Why does Stephen Hawking use a computer?

- ○ Stephen Hawking likes computers.
- ○ The computer lets him speak.
- ○ He is a famous scientist.
- ○ He has written several books.

Hint: A fact is real and true. What is said in the passage?

A sun dog is a bright ring around the sun. Sometimes, the sun dog will also have colors. It may look like a round rainbow. Sun dogs are caused by ice crystals high in the sky. You should never look right at the sun. So wear sunglasses if you want to see a sun dog.

8   Which of these is an OPINION from the passage?

- ○ A sun dog is caused by ice crystals.
- ○ You should not look right at the sun.
- ○ The rainbow colors of a sun dog are beautiful.
- ○ A sun dog is a bright ring around the sun.

Hint: Words that describe are opinion words.

Did you know that your body shrinks as the day goes by? When you wake up, you are at your tallest. Your body is relaxed. Your muscles are stretched, and your joints are loose. As the day passes, your muscles tighten. Gravity pulls down on your body, too. Your body may be an inch shorter by the end of the day.

9   Which of these is a FACT from the passage?

○   When you wake up, you feel good because your body is relaxed.

○   It is good that your muscles tighten so that you don't fall down.

○   Gravity pulls down on your body.

○   It's better to be short than tall.

Hint: Words like "feel good," "it is good," and "it is better" are opinion words.

Have you ever watched a pond freeze in winter? The water freezes first on the top. The ice forms a very thin sheet across the water. It takes only about twenty minutes for this sheet to form. Then slowly the ice begins to grow down toward the bottom. It takes an hour for the first sheet to become two times as thick as it was when it started.

10   Which of these is NOT a fact from the passage?

○   When ice freezes it looks pretty.

○   It takes about twenty minutes for the first sheet of ice to form.

○   It takes an hour for the first sheet to become two times as thick.

○   Ice freezes first on top, forming a very thin sheet across the water.

Hint: Facts are real and true. Which sentence is an opinion?

For years, traveling farm workers were not treated well. At last, Cesar Chavez could stand it no longer. He thought farm workers should be paid more. He wanted better working conditions for them. To gain these, he formed a union. The group went on strike to get what they wanted.

11   Which of these is a FACT from the passage?

○   It was not fair that farm workers were not treated well.

○   Better working conditions mean that farm workers will produce more.

○   To gain better working conditions, Cesar Chavez formed a union.

○   It is not a good idea to go on strike.

Hint: A fact is real and true. What is actually said in the passage?

Objective 4: Summarizing Content

A good summary contains the main idea of a passage. It is short but includes the most important points.

One kind of spider makes a web underwater. It weaves its web in water plants. Then, it carries bubbles of air down to fill the web. The water spider lies still on its web. Soon, a water insect swims near it. The spider dashes out and catches the insect. It brings its catch back to the air-filled web to eat.

1   **Which sentence tells what this story is mostly about?**

   ○   Some spiders look better underwater.

   ○   Water spiders build their webs using air bubbles.

   ○   Water spiders like water insects.

   ○   One kind of spider can live underwater very well.

   Hint: Which sentence tells you about the whole passage?

It is hard to think of doctors as artists. But their job of healing people can be beautiful. For instance, doctors help people who can't hear well. In some cases, doctors use a piece of a rib. They carve the rib so that it fits inside the ear. The bone is about a tenth of an inch high. It also has a pretty and interesting shape. With this bone in the ear, the person can hear much better.

2   **What is the best summary of this passage?**

   ○   Some people think that a doctor is a kind of artist because healing people is beautiful.

   ○   People who can't hear well need to use their ribs to try to hear better.

   ○   Artists know how to carve ribs into pretty shapes.

   ○   Doctors help artists hear better using pieces of ribs.

   Hint: Which sentence tells you about the whole passage?

Calamity Jane was a famous woman of the Wild West. She was famous because she was so tough. She lived during the 1800s. She learned to ride a horse and shoot a gun at an early age. People could always hear her coming. She also liked to dress in men's clothes. There weren't many women like her.

3   What is this story mostly about?

○ It was tough for Calamity Jane to live during the 1800s.

○ Calamity Jane was famous because she was taught to ride a horse.

○ Calamity Jane did things that other women in the 1800s did not.

○ Calamity Jane wore men's clothes.

Hint: Which sentence sums up Calamity Jane?

Cats are very much like lions and tigers. They can jump high in the air. Cats can jump seven feet high. They have padded feet. That way they can sneak up on their prey. Cats have 18 claws on their feet. They can push out and draw back their claws.

4   What is this story mostly about?

○ Cats, lions, and tigers have claws.

○ Cats can jump about seven feet.

○ Cats, lions, and tigers are much alike.

○ Cats quietly sneak up on their prey.

Hint: Which sentence tells you about the whole passage?

Two things make a tree a conifer. One is that it must make seeds in its cones. It must also have needle-like leaves. Conifers are called evergreen trees. They look green all the time. Conifers do lose and replace their leaves. But they never lose all their leaves at the same time.

5   What is this story mostly about?

○ A conifer makes seeds in its cones.

○ A conifer has cones and is an evergreen tree.

○ Evergreen trees look green all the time.

○ Leaves never all fall off at once.

Hint: Which sentence tells you about the whole paragraph?

TEST PRACTICE: SKILL BUILDING

.... **Lesson 1: Reading Comprehension**

Directions: Read each story carefully. Then read each question. Darken the circle for the correct answer.

 More than one answer may seem correct. Choose the answer that goes best with the story.

Sample A

Making Breakfast

Dad and I made our own breakfast. We made pancakes. They tasted better than Mom's pancakes. Dad and I decided we would keep this as our little secret.

Why will they keep the secret?

○ They do not want Mom to know they cooked breakfast.

○ They do not want to hurt Mom's feelings.

○ They burned the pancakes.

 The correct answer is <u>They do not want to hurt Mom's feelings.</u> The story states that the pancakes tasted better than Mom's pancakes. But they will keep this secret. If they tell Mom they might hurt her feelings.

 More than one answer may seem correct. Choose the answer that goes best with the story.

Sample B

Vera and Kit

Vera and Kit were playing. Kit ran to hide. Vera looked for her. Then it began to rain. Vera and Kit got wet. They ran to the house.

What were the girls doing?

○ playing football

○ playing hopscotch

○ playing hide-and-seek

 The correct answer is <u>playing hide-and-seek</u>. The story states that Kit ran to hide. Then Vera looked for her. This is not how to play football. This is not how to play hopscotch.

Directions: Here is a story about a girl named Ava and her donkey. Read this story carefully. Then read each question. Darken the circle for the correct answer.

Ava and Sam

Ava lived in the mountains with her family and a donkey named Sam. Ava and Sam went everywhere together. Sam was a good mountain climber. Ava was not as good at climbing. She had to watch where she walked. When the path was dangerous, Ava would ride on Sam's back. Sam never slipped or fell. He was always careful when Ava was on his back.

Ava rode the donkey on the path down to the stream. There were fish swimming in the stream. Ava and the donkey splashed in the cool, clear water. Later, when they returned home, Ava gave Sam a pail of the food he likes. She brushed his back. Then, Ava went inside for dinner.

Go

1 **Where did Ava and Sam live?**

- ○ on a farm
- ○ in the mountains
- ○ in the city

2 **Why did Ava ride the donkey to the stream?**

- ○ The donkey was tired.
- ○ The path was long.
- ○ The path was dangerous.

3 **How do you know Ava loves Sam?**

- ○ She splashes in the water with him.
- ○ She feeds him the food he likes.
- ○ She rides on his back.

4 Find the picture of Sam.

5 If Sam became sick, what would Ava probably do?

○ She would go to the stream alone.

○ She would find another donkey.

○ She would take care of him.

6 He was always <u>careful</u> when Ava was on his back.

A word that means the | opposite | **of <u>careful</u> is**

○ careless

○ slow

○ watchful

Directions: Here is a story about two sisters. Read this story carefully. Then read each question. Darken the circle for the correct answer.

Big Sister and Little Sister

by Charlotte Zolotow

Once there was a big sister and a little sister. The big sister always took care. Even when she was jumping rope, she took care that her little sister stayed on the sidewalk.

When she rode her bike, she gave her little sister a ride. When she was walking to school, she took little sister's hand and helped her cross the street. When they were playing in the fields, she made sure little sister didn't get lost.

Go

When they were sewing, she made sure little sister's needle was threaded and that little sister held the scissors the right way.

Big sister took care of everything, and little sister thought there was nothing big sister couldn't do.

Little sister would sometimes cry, but big sister always made her stop. First she'd put her arm around her, then she'd hold out her handkerchief and say, "Here, blow."

Big sister knew everything.

"Don't do it like that," she'd say. "Do it this way."

And little sister did. Nothing could bother big sister. She knew too much.

But one day little sister wanted to be alone. She was tired of big sister saying, "Sit here."

"Go there."

"Do it this way."

"Come along."

7 **Little sister thought that big sister**

- ○ knew nothing
- ○ knew everything
- ○ didn't care

8 **What is something big sister did <u>not</u> do?**

- ○ give little sister a ride
- ○ take care of little sister
- ○ listen to little sister

9 **Why did little sister get tired of big sister?**

- ○ She liked to be told what to do.
- ○ She didn't want to sit down.
- ○ She wanted to be on her own.

10 **What did little sister probably do next?**

- ○ keep listening to big sister
- ○ run away from big sister
- ○ get big sister to listen to her

11 **Nothing could <u>bother</u> big sister.**

Another word for <u>bother</u> is

- ○ trouble
- ○ please
- ○ calm

Directions: Read this poem about two kittens carefully. Then read each question. Darken the circle for the correct answer.

TWO LITTLE KITTENS

Two little kittens, one stormy night,

    Began to hiss, and then to fight;

One had a mouse, the other had none,

    And that's the way the fight begun.

"I'll have that mouse," said the biggest cat;

    "You'll have that mouse? We'll see about that!"

"I'll have that mouse," said the oldest son;

    "You won't have the mouse," said the little one.

I told you before it was a stormy night,

    When these two little kittens began to fight;

The old woman grabbed her sweeping broom,

    And swept the two kittens right out of the room.

The ground was covered with ice and snow,

    And the two little kittens had nowhere to go;

So they laid themselves down on the mat at the door,

    While the old woman finished sweeping the floor.

Then they crept in, as quiet as mice,

    All wet with snow, and cold as ice,

For they found it was better, that stormy night,

    To lie down and sleep than to hiss and fight.

12 Why were the two kittens fighting?

- ○ They did not want to share the mouse.
- ○ One kitten wanted to let the mouse go.
- ○ They did not like each other.
- ○ One kitten wanted to sleep alone.

13 Why does the old woman sweep the kittens outside?

- ○ She does not want them to fight.
- ○ She is cleaning the house.
- ○ They do not belong in the house.
- ○ They sleep on the mat at the door.

14 What lesson did the kittens learn?

- ○ You should be quiet.
- ○ You should go to sleep.
- ○ You should not be greedy.
- ○ You should not eat mice.

15 What most likely happened to the mouse?

- ○ The biggest cat got it.
- ○ It ran away when the kittens started to fight.
- ○ The littlest cat got it.
- ○ It crept into the house with the kittens.

STOP

Directions: Read the story carefully. Then read the question. Darken the circle for the correct answer.

Sample A

Celina's Vacation Plans

Celina is excited about going camping with her family this summer. They plan to go to the Grand Canyon where they will stay for two weeks.

How long will Celina's family camp?

○ two days

○ two weeks

○ the entire summer

Directions: Here is a poem about a place to rest. Read this poem. Then read each question. Darken the circle for the correct answer.

Comfortable Old Chair

by Karla Kuskin

A bird has a nest
    A fox has a lair
A den is home
    If you're a bear.
I have a comfortable old chair.

Soft pillowed blue,
    a flowered cloud.
The perfect place to read aloud
    to myself or silently
letting long words run over me,
    letting the stories I have read
make moving pictures in my head.
    New chairs are nice
but mine is best.

My spot to think in
brood in
rest
to plot in
dream in, many dreams,
to scheme a few outlandish schemes in.
Kings need crowns to be the king
but me
I can be anything
any person
anywhere
if I just have my book and chair.

brood = worry

plot = plan

scheme = plan

1 What does a bear call home?

2 **How does the poet feel when she's in her chair?**

○ unhappy

○ at home

○ lonely

3 **The poet wrote**

letting the stories I have read
make <u>moving pictures</u> in my head.

What are the <u>moving pictures</u>?

○ movies

○ books

○ thoughts

4 **What kind of person is the poet?**

○ a dreamer

○ a king

○ a lazy person

5 **What would happen if the poet's chair ripped?**

○ She would buy a new one.

○ She would throw it out.

○ She would fix the rip.

Directions: Here is a tale about a boy and two giants. Read this tale. Then read each question. Darken the circle for the correct answer.

Sammy Small and the Giants

Sammy Small's mother was leaving the house. "Now," she directed her son, "don't leave the house."

"Why not?" Sammy asked.

"The giant Sneezy Snatcher will grab you," said his mother.

Sammy didn't believe in Sneezy Snatcher. So, as soon as his mother left the house, Sammy left too.

But Sneezy Snatcher was real. And just then he was standing by Sammy's house with a sack over his shoulder. Sneezy picked Sammy up with just two fingers. Sammy squealed and squirmed, but it did no good. Sneezy Snatcher dropped him into the sack.

When Sneezy got home, he called his wife, who was also a giant. "Look love," he said. "I caught a boy we can have for dinner. You watch him while I go out and get a few vegetables to put in the pot with him."

After Sneezy left, Sammy sat on the table looking at Mrs. Snatcher. She looked so silly that Sammy began to build up his courage. "Does Mr. Snatcher ever eat anything but boys?" he finally asked. "Does he sometimes have pudding for dessert?"

"Sneezy and I just love pudding," Mrs. Snatcher said. "But we don't have it often. These are bad times for us giants."

"My mom made a great big pudding this morning," Sammy said. "It's got lots of raisins in it."

"Mmmm," said Mrs. Snatcher. "That sounds delicious."

"I know Mom would be happy to give you some," said Sammy. "Shall I run home and get some from her?"

"You are a generous boy," said Mrs. Snatcher. "By all means, go home. But be sure to hurry back because I'll need time to boil you for dinner."

"I'll be as fast as lightning," Sammy promised. And he did run home as fast as lightning. But you can be sure that he didn't go back to be boiled. Sammy lived happily ever after because he never went out of the house without his mother again.

6 Why was Sammy caught by the giant?

○ He didn't listen to his mother.

○ He was good to eat.

○ He stole the pudding for dessert.

7 Why was Sneezy Snatcher able to pick Sammy up with just two fingers?

○ Sammy was a little boy.

○ Sneezy Snatcher was huge.

○ Sammy didn't fight back.

8 How does Sammy feel at the end of the tale?

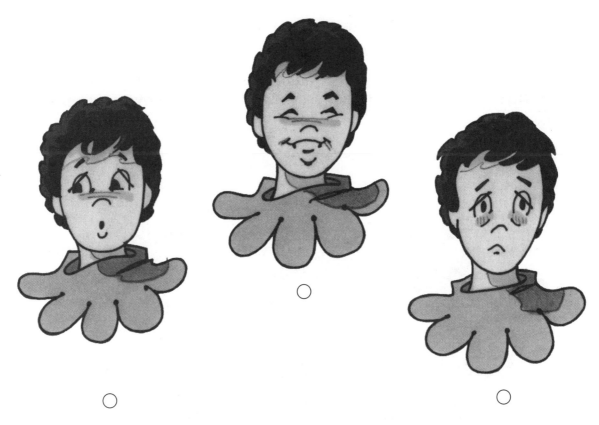

9 How do we know that Mrs. Snatcher wasn't too smart?

○ She liked pudding for dessert.

○ She looked silly.

○ She let Sammy go home to get the pudding.

Directions: Here is a story about a famous American. Read the story. Then read each question. Darken the circle for the correct answer.

Johnny Appleseed

The next time you bite into a crisp, red, juicy apple, remember the name John Chapman. John Chapman, perhaps better known as Johnny Appleseed, planted many apple trees in early America.

Johnny was born in Massachusetts during the Revolutionary War. When he grew up, he traveled west. He planted apple trees wherever he went. Johnny helped the new settlers who were moving to the West during this time. He gave apple seeds and young apple trees to them.

Johnny was well-liked because of all his good deeds. He made friends with both settlers and Native Americans. Many stories, poems, and plays have been written about him. It is said that he had a pet wolf and slept in a treetop. We don't know how many of these stories are true. But we do know that Johnny Appleseed helped many people.

10 **Why is John Chapman better known as Johnny Appleseed?**

○ The name Appleseed tells you what he did.

○ He liked to eat apples.

○ An apple was named after him.

○ People could not remember the name Chapman.

11 **In the story you get the idea that Johnny Appleseed**

○ was not a real person

○ was a very special person

○ was not very smart

○ was an unhappy person

12 **Johnny was well-liked because of all his <u>good deeds</u>.**

What does the phrase <u>good deeds</u> mean?

○ friendliness

○ apple seeds

○ acts to help others

○ worthwhile lessons

13 **The apples show some things we know about Johnny Appleseed.**

planted apple trees

traveled west

made many friends

Find the sentence that goes in the empty apple.

○ was born in Massachusetts

○ wrote many stories, poems, plays

○ had a pet wolf

○ slept in a treetop

Directions: This article tells you about what some animals do in winter. Read the article carefully. Then read each question. Darken the circle for the correct answer.

THE DEEP SLEEPERS

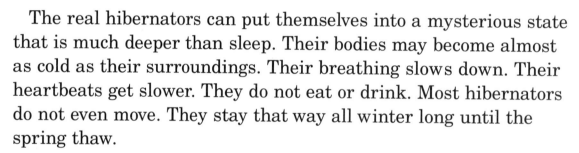

In many places, winter is a tough time for animals. Snow covers the ground, and food is hard to find. Some animals sleep through the coldest months, but only a few can really hibernate.

Many people think that bears hibernate, but this is not true. Bears make a bed under a ledge or in a cave. Then they go to sleep when it gets cold. They may arise and move around during warm days.

The real hibernators can put themselves into a mysterious state that is much deeper than sleep. Their bodies may become almost as cold as their surroundings. Their breathing slows down. Their heartbeats get slower. They do not eat or drink. Most hibernators do not even move. They stay that way all winter long until the spring thaw.

The ground squirrel is probably the best hibernator of all. Throughout the summer, he stuffs himself with food. He will live off stored body fat for eight months.

When autumn comes, the ground squirrel digs a little burrow three feet under the ground. The temperature will always be the same there, even if it is freezing up above. The squirrel crawls into his little hole and rolls up into a tight ball. Ever so slowly, his heartbeat begins to slow down. It goes from 300 beats a minute to just five! The squirrel's body temperature falls from 95°F to 35°F. Nobody knows how the ground squirrel can do this, but it works every time.

Hibernation is a big mystery. Scientists are not sure just how animals do it. But they would like to find out.

14 What is the author's MAIN purpose in writing this passage?

- ○ to explain what happens when an animal hibernates
- ○ to make the reader want to help animals
- ○ to entertain the reader with strange animal stories
- ○ to explain how a ground squirrel stores fat

15 Why is winter a difficult time for some animals?

- ○ it rains too much
- ○ food is hard to find
- ○ there isn't a lot of sunlight
- ○ it gets dark early

16 Which does NOT happen when animals hibernate?

- ○ Their heartbeats get slower.
- ○ They go outside to find food.
- ○ Their breathing slows down.
- ○ They don't eat or drink.

17 Why do people think that bears hibernate?

- ○ They sleep a lot in the summer.
- ○ They are found in a mysterious state.
- ○ They move around on warm days.
- ○ They sleep a lot in the winter.

· · · · · · · · · · ## Lesson 2: Sentence Structure

Directions: Read each sample. Darken the circle for the correct answer.

 Pretend that you are writing this sentence. Choose the words that belong in the blanks. Think of the rules you have learned.

Sample A

My dog _____.

- ○ running and barking
- ○ long brown hair
- ○ is my best friend

 The correct answer is <u>is my best friend</u>. A complete sentence needs a subject and a verb. In this sentence, the subject is "My dog." The verb must agree with the subject. The verb "is" agrees with "My dog."

 Choose the answer carefully. Try each one in the sentence. Only one is correct. Pick the answer that belongs.

Sample B

This story is _____ than that one.

- ○ interesting
- ○ more interesting
- ○ most interesting

 The correct answer is <u>more interesting</u>. This is the only answer that fits in the sentence.

Directions: Choose the word or words that belong in the blanks.

1 In the morning, I _____ down what I dreamed the night before.

- ○ writing
- ○ write
- ○ writes

September 8, 2002

_(2)_

I read a good story about sisters. I should be nicer to my little sister. Are you nice to your little sister?

_(3)_

Simon

2
- ○ dear maria,
- ○ Dear maria,
- ○ Dear Maria,

3
- ○ Your Cousin,
- ○ Your cousin,
- ○ your cousin,

4 I can be anything if I _____.

- ○ work at it
- ○ always have
- ○ flying with the birds
- ○ not act lazy

5 **Choose the subject of the sentence. Darken the circle for the correct answer.**

<u>Brenda and her mom</u> will go camping <u>this fall</u> with <u>her cousin Donna</u>.
      ○   ○   ○

STOP

Lesson 3: Writing Strategies

Directions: Read each sample. Darken the circle for the correct answer.

 Choose the sentence that best completes the story. Try each answer in place of the missing sentence. Only one belongs in the story. Pick the one that makes the most sense in the story.

Sample A

I have a chair in my room. I am not happy when I sit in it. _____.

○ I can see the park across the street.

○ It is where I do my homework.

○ My desk is next to the chair.

○ It feels nice and soft.

 The correct answer is <u>It is where I do my homework</u>. This is the only sentence that can go at the end of this story. The other answers do not explain why the author does not like to sit in his chair.

 Choose the best topic sentence for this story. Pick the answer that tells the main idea of the story. Try that answer in place of the missing sentence.

Sample B

_____. She sorts the clothes before they are washed. She cleans out the bird's cage.

○ Cindy helps her father with the housework.

○ Cindy likes to wash the clothes.

○ Cindy lives in a big house.

○ Cindy is eight years old.

 The correct answer is <u>Cindy helps her father with the housework</u>. This is the only sentence that tells the main idea of the story. The other answers tell about Cindy. But they do not tell about the story.

Directions: Choose the sentence that best completes the story.

1   **Mr. Han asked Ned to do some jobs. _____. Mr. Han always gives him a dollar for each job.**

○ Ned asked Mr. Han if he could work for him.

○ Ned is lazy and does not like to work.

○ Ned told him that he could not help.

○ Ned is a hard worker.

2   **On rainy days, I sit in my chair and read. _____.**

○ I play all day. My friends and I play fun games.

○ I like to read fairy tales the best. I dream I'm a queen.

○ I watch TV every day. My mother does not like that.

○ I am a very good soccer player. I am on a team.

Directions: Choose the best topic sentence for the story.

3   **_____. The farm is five miles from his school. He rides a bus to school because he lives too far to walk.**

○ Michael lives on a farm.

○ Michael is in third grade.

○ Michael likes to walk to school.

○ Michael's father is a farmer.

4   **_____. The number of rings tells a tree's age. The more rings you count, the older the tree is.**

○ Each ring stands for a year of growth.

○ Tree rings are narrow near the center.

○ After a tree is cut down, you can see rings on the stump.

○ You might see many rings.

Lesson 4: Editing Skills

Directions: Read each sample. Darken the circle for the correct answer.

Try This Choose the sentence that is written correctly. Think of the rules you have learned. Pick the sentence that follows all the rules.

Sample A

○ Her and me went to the movies.

○ My sister and I play together.

○ Us are good friends.

○ Them kids like to watch television.

The correct answer is <u>My sister and I play together</u>. This is the only sentence with the correct pronouns.

Try This Choose the sentence that has the correct capitalization and punctuation. Pick the sentence that follows all the rules.

Sample B

○ The bird began to sing

○ the sound it made was beautiful.

○ I was very quiet?

○ I didn't want the bird to stop.

The correct answer is <u>I didn't want the bird to stop</u>. The sentence begins with a capital letter and ends with a period.

Directions: Choose the word that can take the place of the underlined word.

1   **Whales** can be found in all oceans of the world.

   ○ He
   ○ She
   ○ It
   ○ They

Directions: Choose the sentence that is written correctly.

2   ○ Hanging from the apple tree.
    ○ Flying through the night.
    ○ Hunting for the fox.
    ○ Flying through the air is fun.

3   ○ The rain were falling.
    ○ The rain rolled down the roof.
    ○ The rain made many trees to falled to earth.
    ○ We hasn't seen so much rain in a long time.

Directions: Choose the sentence that has the correct capitalization and punctuation.

4   ○ She likes to sit in her old chair.
    ○ She looks out the window!
    ○ she watches the clouds float by.
    ○ That is where she dreams

5   ○ Bear dens are not usually found in new Orleans, Louisiana.
    ○ You might see a bear in the mountains of idaho.
    ○ Polar bears live in Barrow Alaska.
    ○ You would not see a bear on the streets of New York City.

Directions: Choose the word that belongs in the blank. Darken the circle for the correct answer.

Sample A

After Natasha _____ the song, everyone clapped.

○ sing

○ singing

○ sang

Directions: Here is a story about an important food. Read this story. Then read each question. Darken the circle for the correct answer.

Bread

When you think of bread, what comes to mind? Do you think of a piece of white bread? If you lived in another country, you might have a very different idea of bread. A boy or girl in Mexico would think of tortillas. These are flat, round breads made from corn. People in India would think of chappatis. These are heavy pieces of round bread that are fried.

Bread is one of the most important foods. It is eaten more than any other food. It is also eaten in more places around the world than any other food.

The first bread was made about 12,000 years ago. People in the Middle East used seeds to make flour. They mixed the flour with water. Then they baked it on hot rocks.

Later, people in Egypt added something called yeast. Yeast made the bread rise. The Egyptians also built ovens. For hundreds of years, bread has been made in the same way.

Directions: Choose the words that belong in the blanks.

1 _____ bakes bread.

- ○ A baker
- ○ The first bread
- ○ In the oven

I love to eat bread. I __(2)__ Italian bread the best. I put a
lot of butter on a slice __(3)__ I eat it!

2 ○ eat
   ○ bake
   ○ like

3 ○ after
   ○ before
   ○ to

Directions: Here is a story a student wrote about his father. The student made some mistakes. Read this story carefully. Then read each question. Darken the circle for the correct answer.

[1.] My dad was a young boy when he came to America. [2.] He life was never very easy. [3.] He started to worked before he was eight years old. [4.] My dad always worked hard. [5.] That is why he became a success. [6.] One day he opening a clothing store. [7.] Soon he have many stores. [8.] He made the American dream come true.

4   Choose the best way to write sentence 2.

○   His life was never very easy.

○   Him life was never very easy.

○   Its life was never very easy.

○   It is best as it is.

5   Choose the best way to write sentence 3.

○   He started to working before he was eight years old.

○   He started to works before he was eight years old.

○   He started to work before he was eight years old.

○   It is best as it is.

6   Choose the best way to write sentence 6.

○   Opening a clothing store one day.

○   One day he opened a clothing store.

○   He opening a clothing store one day.

○   It is best as it is.

7   Choose the best way to write sentence 7.

○   Soon he had many stores.

○   Soon he having many stores.

○   Soon he haded many stores.

○   It is best as it is.

Directions: Here is a story about Kristi Yamaguchi, a figure-skating star. Read this story carefully. Then read each question. Darken the circle for the correct answer.

Skating for Gold

The year 1992 was a good one for Kristi Yamaguchi. That year she won gold medals in the United States and World figure-skating contests. In the 1992 Winter Olympics, she won gold for the United States. Three medals in one year!

Kristi is awesome! She twists and turns. She flies through the air. It's hard to believe that Kristi was born with a turned-in foot. She had to wear special shoes. They helped her foot stay straight. When she was four years old, her parents sent her to dance lessons. They thought dancing would help her walk better. They thought it would make her legs strong. When she was six, she started skating lessons. Even at six, Kristi skated great.

United States skater Dorothy Hamill won a gold medal in the 1976 Olympics. That was one year before Kristi started skating. Dorothy was Kristi's hero. Kristi says, "Every little girl wanted to be just like Dorothy." Kristi wanted to be like Dorothy, too.

All Kristi's hard work paid off in 1992. She became a gold medal winner just like her hero. Kristi Yamaguchi has lived her dream.

8 **A student found out more about Kristi Yamaguchi. Choose the best topic sentence for her story.**

_____. When she was training, Kristi had to get up at 4 A.M. She practiced skating before school. She also went to a dance class once a week.

- ○ Kristi worked hard to be a winner.
- ○ Kristi admired Dorothy Hamill.
- ○ Kristi always wanted to ice skate.
- ○ Kristi grew up in California.

9 **Choose the sentence that is written correctly.**

- ○ To win the contest.
- ○ Dancing to music.
- ○ The ice is very slippery.
- ○ Ice skating always fun.

10 **Choose the sentence that best completes the story.**

Figure skating is done on a large, egg-shaped rink. _____. Each skater takes a turn skating around the ice.

- ○ They all do jumps and turns.
- ○ Music is played.
- ○ The fans clapped after every jump.
- ○ It takes years of practice to be in the Olympics.

11 Choose the word that is the subject of the sentence.

The <u>skater</u> is the most <u>important</u> <u>person</u> on the <u>ice</u>.

    ○   ○   ○   ○

Directions: Choose the words that belong in the blanks.

> November 22, 2002
>
> (12)
> _____
>
> It was fun reading about Kristi Yamaguchi. Now I want to learn how to skate. Would you like to borrow my book?
>
> (13)
> _____
> Lucia

12 ○ dear carol,
    ○ Dear Carol,
    ○ Dear carol
    ○ Dear Carol

13 ○ Your Friend
    ○ your friend,
    ○ Your friend,
    ○ Your friend

·········· **Lesson 5: Number and Number Relations**

Directions: Read each question carefully. Darken the circle for the correct answer.

 When reading word names for numbers, imagine filling in the number from left to right.

Sample

Which of these is three hundred six?

○ 36

○ 360

○ 306

○ 603

 The correct answer is 306. Since there are no tens, a zero goes in the tens place.

---

1   **What number is shown by the blocks in the picture below?**

○ 407

○ 47

○ 74

○ 704

2   **Jan had the highest score on her bowling team last week. What was Jan's score?**

○ 128

○ 140

○ 134

○ 143

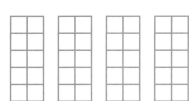

Last Week's
Bowling Scores
———
105
128
140
116
98
134

STOP

Directions: Read each question carefully. Darken the circle for the correct answer.

Try This Read word problems carefully. This helps you understand exactly what is being asked for.

Sample

In Ms. Royster's class, the students have 17 pet dogs and 14 pet cats. How many pet dogs and cats are there in all?

- ○ 31
- ○ 21
- ○ 41
- ○ 184
- ○ None of these

Think It Through The correct answer is <u>31</u>. To find the total number of pets, add the number of dogs and the number of cats. $17 + 14 = \underline{31}$.

---

1 $9 + 6 =$

- ○ 96
- ○ 63
- ○ 56
- ○ 54
- ○ None of these

2 Tom bought three items at a baseball game. Which amount is closest to the amount Tom spent?

- ○ $40
- ○ $30
- ○ $20
- ○ $10

PLAYERS YEARBOOK

GO TEAM

○ **$6.00**   ○ **$2.00**   ○ **$9.00**

STOP

Lesson 7: Operation Concepts

Directions: Read each question carefully. Darken the circle for the correct answer.

 Read the directions for the problem carefully. Then try each of the answers in the problem.

Sample

Look at the number sentence below. Which number in the box makes it true?

 The correct answer is 8, since $4 + 8 = 12$.

$4 + \square = 12$

- ○ 4
- ○ 6
- ○ 8
- ○ 10

---

1 Ian and Sharon bought two pizzas. They carried them home. On the way, they ate three slices. How many slices were left when they got home?

- ○ 17
- ○ 15
- ○ 13
- ○ 5

2 Bob bought an apple for 40 cents and a roll for 30 cents. Which number sentence shows what he spent in all?

- ○ $40 + 30 = 70$
- ○ $40 - 30 = 10$
- ○ $30 + 10 = 40$
- ○ $10 + 30 = 40$

Lesson 8: Measurement

Directions: Read each question carefully. Darken the circle for the correct answer.

> **Try This** When counting time on a clock, try to picture the minute hand moving forward. This can help you keep track of minutes.

Sample

The clock shows the time it is now. How many minutes are there until the minute hand reaches the 10?

○ 50 minutes
○ 25 minutes
○ 10 minutes
○ 5 minutes

 **Think It Through** The correct answer is <u>25 minutes</u>. The minute hand is now on the 5. As it moves forward, each number reached means that five minutes have passed. To get to 10, it goes past 5 numbers. 5 x 5 = 25 minutes.

---

1 Use the centimeter side of your ruler to solve this problem.

What is the length of the longer side of the rectangle?

○ 3 cm
○ 4 cm
○ 5 cm
○ 6 cm

2 Which is most likely measured in inches?

○ the amount of juice in a cup
○ the weight of a piano
○ the width of a photo
○ the height of a tall building

Directions: Read each question carefully. Darken the circle for the correct answer.

 When you are asked how a figure changes, draw it on paper. Fold it, turn it, or slide it.

Sample

Georgia flipped the figure over the line shown. What figure did she get?

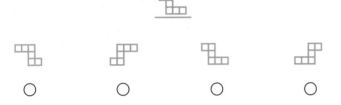

○   ○   ○   ○

Think It Through  The correct answer is ⌐╝. When a figure is flipped over a line below it, top becomes bottom and bottom becomes top.

---

1   **Which two figures are the same?**

   ○ R and U
   ○ T and V
   ○ V and S
   ○ S and U

2   **Which figure has four sides that are the same length?**

   ○ circle
   ○ triangle
   ○ rectangle
   ○ square

Lesson 10: Data Analysis, Statistics, and Probability

Directions: Read each question carefully. Darken the circle for the correct answer.

Try This

Always read problems carefully. Make sure you understand the question. Or else, you may give the wrong answer!

Sample

Todd spun the spinner shown. Which number does he have the best chance of landing on?

○ 1
○ 2
○ 3
○ 4

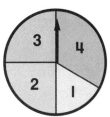

Think It Through

The correct answer is <u>4</u>. The spinner has the best chance of landing on the number with the largest space. The number 4 is in the largest space.

Some students were asked how many telephones they had at home. Study the graph and use it to answer problems 1 and 2.

How many phones do you have at home?

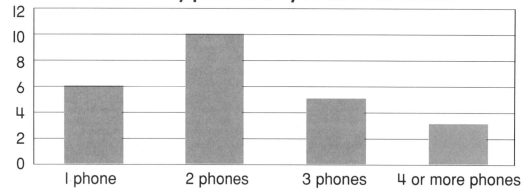

1 How many students have 2 telephones at home?

○ 10 students
○ 16 students
○ 15 students
○ 12 students

2 How many students were asked about telephones?

○ 10
○ 14
○ 24
○ 25

STOP

Directions: Read each question carefully. Darken the circle for the correct answer.

 This question asks about a pattern. See how you can get from the first number to the next. See if you can use the same rule for the next numbers.

Sample

Look at the pattern below. What number comes next?

40, 60, 80, 100, ___

○ 101
○ 110
○ 120
○ 180

 **Think It Through** The correct answer is 120. 40 + 20 = 60. 60 + 20 = 80. 100 + 20 = 120.

---

1 **How many squares will there be in the next figure of the pattern?**

○ 25
○ 16
○ 13
○ 10

 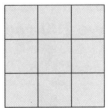 **?**

_____

2 **Today's date is Wednesday, May 9. Felo's birthday is two weeks from this Friday. When is Felo's birthday?**

○ May 11
○ May 18
○ May 23
○ May 25

~ May ~						
S	M	T	W	T	F	S
		1	2	3	4	5
6	7	8	9	10	11	12
13	14	15	16	17	18	19
20	21	22	23	24	25	26
27	28	29	30	31		

STOP

Lesson 12: Problem Solving and Reasoning

Directions: Read each question carefully. Darken the circle for the correct answer.

 Test each answer listed. This will help you get rid of incorrect answers.

Sample

Abe has an even number of quarters in his pocket. How much money could he have in quarters?

- ○ $0.75
- ○ $0.80
- ○ $0.90
- ○ $1.00

 The correct answer is $1.00. Abe could have 4 quarters totaling $1.00. Choice A does not work. 3 quarters total $0.75 and 3 is an odd number. Choices B and C do not work. You cannot make those amounts with quarters.

---

1 Every morning Peter adds 5 rocks to his rock garden. Every evening a squirrel hides one of the rocks. How many days will it take Peter to have 100 rocks in his rock garden?

- ○ 20 days
- ○ 24 days
- ○ 25 days
- ○ 100 days

2 Coco bought two large pieces of chalk. She received the change shown from a $1 bill.

How much did each piece of chalk cost?

- ○ 19 cents
- ○ 14 cents
- ○ 24 cents
- ○ 31 cents

Lesson 13: Communication

Directions: Read each question carefully. Darken the circle for the correct answer.

 Try This

Look at the picture carefully. Make sure you understand all the information in it.

Sample

Tasha is 11 years old. How much will it cost for Tasha and her mother to attend a movie?

○ $16
○ $14
○ $8
○ $6

Movie Ticket Prices

Children (under age 12) $6

Adults $8

 **Think It Through**

The correct answer is $14. Since Tasha is under age 12, she pays $6. Her mother pays $8. In all, they pay $6 + $8 = $14.

---

1   How far is it from Pocaville to Wimlette along Route 64?

○ 92 miles
○ 82 miles
○ 47 miles
○ 45 miles

Route 64	
West	**East**
←	→
Pocaville	Wimlette
45 miles	47 miles

2   Pia starts at her house. She walks three blocks south. Then she walks two blocks west. Where is she now?

○ at the school
○ at the park
○ at the pet shop
○ at the bus stop

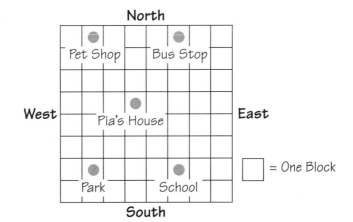

Directions: Read each question carefully. Darken the circle for the correct answer.

1   38 + 7 =
   ○ 35
   ○ 45
   ○ 108
   ○ 315
   ○ None of these

2   4 × 8 =
   ○ 12
   ○ 24
   ○ 36
   ○ 48
   ○ None of these

3   68 − 5 =
   ○ 63
   ○ 73
   ○ 18
   ○ 62
   ○ None of these

4   **Thomas bought a packet of seeds for $0.79 and a pencil for $0.55. How much did he spend in all?**
   ○ $1.34
   ○ $1.33
   ○ $1.24
   ○ $1.23
   ○ None of these

5 Ursula had the pennies shown below. She gave three of the pennies to her friend, Wei. What number sentence tells how many pennies Ursula had left?

○ 7 + 3 = 10
○ 6 + 3 = 9
○ 6 – 3 = 3
○ 7 – 3 = 4

6 Arnold has two dollars. Which item can he __not__ buy?

○ box of crayons
○ ball
○ bag of potato chips
○ box of cookies

$1.89 $1.29   89¢ $2.19

7 Which number is 306 + 387 closest to?

○ 600
○ 700
○ 800
○ 900

8 What number is missing in the number pattern?

50, 100, 150, ___, 250

○ 300
○ 200
○ 151
○ 160

9 **What number is shown by the blocks in the picture below?**

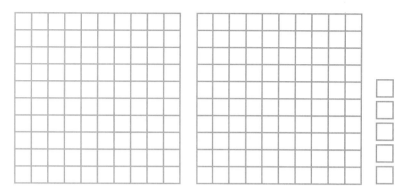

- ○ 250
- ○ 205
- ○ 52
- ○ 25

10 **In the number 4,067 which place holds a zero?**

- ○ ones
- ○ tens
- ○ hundreds
- ○ thousands

11 **Use the centimeter side of your ruler. What is the length of the figure's longest side?**

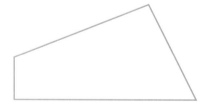

- ○ 5 centimeters
- ○ 4 centimeters
- ○ 3 centimeters
- ○ 2 centimeters

12 Which figure comes next in the pattern?

● □ ○ ■ ● □ ○ ■ ●

- ○ ●
- ○ □
- ○ ○
- ○ ■

13 Which would you use to measure weight?

- ○ inch
- ○ cup
- ○ kilometer
- ○ pound

14 Steven has to choose the number he thinks the spinner will land on. Which number should he choose?

- ○ 1
- ○ 2
- ○ 3
- ○ 4

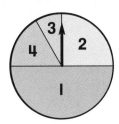

15 Janet has two coins in her pocket. Which amount could she <u>not</u> have?

- ○ 26 cents
- ○ 20 cents
- ○ 15 cents
- ○ 7 cents

16 **Which number is the same as eight thousand six hundred forty?**

- ○ 864
- ○ 8,064
- ○ 8,604
- ○ 8,640

17 **Which number sentence has an answer smaller than 10?**

- ○ 10 − 0 = ___
- ○ 10 − 5 = ___
- ○ 10 + 0 = ___
- ○ 10 + 5 = ___

18 **Look at the clock. How many minutes are there until 6:00?**

- ○ 9 minutes
- ○ 25 minutes
- ○ 45 minutes
- ○ 1 hour

19 **What is the shape of the street sign?**

- ○ circle
- ○ square
- ○ rectangle
- ○ triangle

Name the Iguana

Directions: A class had a pet iguana. They picked four names. Then everyone picked the name they liked best. What they picked is shown in the graph below. Use the graph to answer problems 20 through 22.

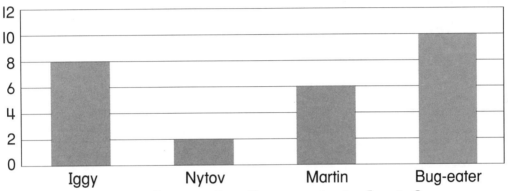

20 Which name was chosen by the most students?

- ○ Iggy
- ○ Nytov
- ○ Martin
- ○ Bug-eater

21 How many more students chose Martin than chose Nytov?

- ○ 2
- ○ 4
- ○ 6
- ○ 8

22 The next day three students who picked Bug-eater changed their mind. They decided they liked Nytov better. What is the winning name now?

- ○ Iggy
- ○ Nytov
- ○ Martin
- ○ Bug-eater

23 On her way to school, Dana found three pennies near her house. Then she found five nickels at the bus stop. On the bus she found a quarter and a dime. How would you find the number of coins she found in all?

- ○ add
- ○ divide
- ○ multiply
- ○ subtract

24 Which two figures are the same shape and the same size?

| 1 | 2 | 3 |

| 4 | 5 | 6 |

- ○ 1 and 5
- ○ 2 and 6
- ○ 2 and 4
- ○ 2 and 3

25 Kyle's dog, Barkum, is 6 years old. If he were a person, how old would he be? Follow the directions below.

> ### A Dog's Age
>
> 1. Find how old your dog is.
>
> 2. Multiply the number of years by 7.
>
> 3. The answer is your dog's age if he were a person.

- ○ 13 years old
- ○ 35 years old
- ○ 42 years old
- ○ 49 years old

Sample A

Brooke ate breakfast. She went out the door. She waited for the school bus. When the bus came, Brooke climbed aboard.

Find the picture that shows where Brooke was going.

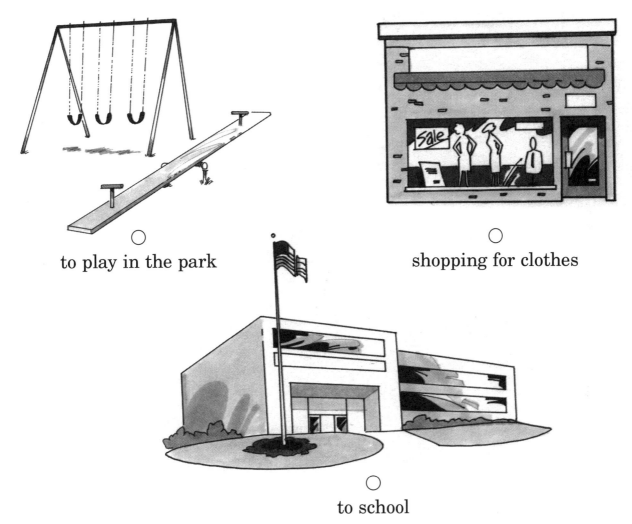

○ to play in the park

○ shopping for clothes

○ to school

Sample B

Choose the words that belong in the blank.

My house _____.

○ and my father

○ painting yellow

○ is two-stories high

○ very comfortable

STOP

Part 1

Make-Believe

It's fun to make-believe. You can be anything you want to be. It's fun to read stories that are make-believe, too.

First, you will read a poem about a boy who pretends. Then you will read some stories about things that are not real.

Directions: Here is a poem about a boy who makes-believe while he is sick. Read this poem carefully. Then read each question. Darken the circle for the correct answer.

The Land of Counterpane

by Robert Louis Stevenson

counterpane = bedspread or quilt

When I was sick and lay in bed,
  I had two pillows at my head,
And all my toys beside me lay,
  To keep me happy all the day.

And sometimes for an hour or so,
  I watched my toy soldiers go,
With different uniforms and drills.
  Among the bed-clothes, through the hills.

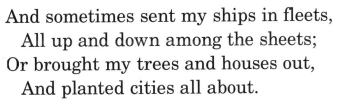

And sometimes sent my ships in fleets,
  All up and down among the sheets;
Or brought my trees and houses out,
  And planted cities all about.

I was the giant great and still,
  That sits upon the pillow hill,
And sees before him valley and plain,
  The pleasant land of counterpane.

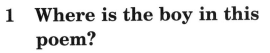

1 Where is the boy in this poem?

○ in a place called Counterpane

○ in his bed

○ in the countryside

2 Which of these ideas from the poem are real?

○ The boy is a giant.

○ The boy plants trees.

○ The boy has a set of toy ships.

Go

3   Find the picture that shows how the boy feels.

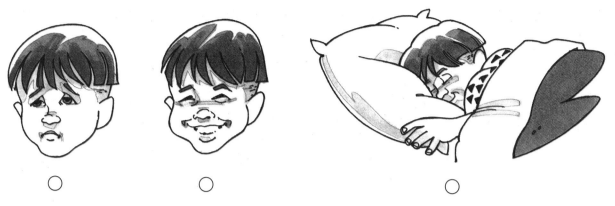

○   ○   ○

4   How does the boy think of his toys?

○   The toys are real things.

○   The toys don't work very well.

○   The toys are old.

5   I watched my toy soldiers <u>go</u>.

A word that means the boxed opposite **of <u>go</u> is**

○   stay

○   leave

○   move

6   Choose the words that belong in the blank.

Our soldiers _____.

○   going home

○   climb the hills

○   on the bed

7   Find the word that can take the place of the boy in the sentence below.

<u>The boy</u> played with his toys in bed.

○   He

○   She

○   It

Directions: Here is a story about a parrot. Read this story carefully. Then read each question. Darken the circle for the correct answer.

THE GREEN CHICKEN

perch = a resting place

by Alvin Schwartz

parrot = a bird

Jill's friend left his parrot, Edward, with her for a few days. Jill put Edward's perch in a sunny window in the kitchen. It was a pleasant place for him to rest. She fastened a long, thin chain to one of his legs so that he could fly when he wanted to, but could not fly away.

Edward had learned to speak a few words his owners had taught him. "Good morning!" he would croak. "Have you had your breakfast yet? Have a bit of buttered toast. It's awfully good."

peering = looking

But at Jill's house, Edward had nothing to say. He sat quietly on his perch looking this way and that, his big golden eyes peering sadly out of his bright-green feathers.

"What is that hairy thing in the corner?" he asked himself. It was Jill's cat, Beatrice, staring at him.

"Whatever can that be?" Beatrice thought. "Oh, of course. It is a green chicken. How delicious it looks!"

Edward stared back at Beatrice. "That is an enemy," he told himself. He ruffled his feathers, rattled his chain, tapped his bill nervously on his perch, and waited.

Go

Beatrice crept out of the corner, her body pressed to the floor, her tiny yellow eyes fixed on Edward. Edward watched anxiously, raising first one foot, then the other.

Suddenly Beatrice sprang into the air and landed next to him.

"Good morning," Edward cried out in fright. "Have you had your breakfast yet?" Beatrice was so startled she fell off the perch and landed on her head.

"Have a piece of buttered toast," Edward croaked. "It's awfully good."

"It's not a green chicken," Beatrice thought. "It's a green person!" She ran from the room and didn't go near Edward again.

8 Jill's friend left Edward with Jill because

○ Edward was lonely

○ Edward needed a baby sitter

○ Edward needed speaking lessons

9 Why did Edward have a chain around his leg?

○ to keep him from falling off the perch

○ to keep him quiet

○ to keep him from flying away

10 What did Beatrice think Edward was?

- ○ a parrot
- ○ a chicken
- ○ a cat

11 At the end why did Beatrice think Edward was a person?

- ○ Edward ate buttered toast.
- ○ Edward knocked her off the perch.
- ○ Edward spoke to her.

12 Suddenly Beatrice <u>sprang</u> into the air.

Another word for <u>sprang</u> is

- ○ jumped
- ○ sang
- ○ ran

13 The window was a <u>pleasant</u> place to rest.

A word that means the |opposite| **of <u>pleasant</u> is**

- ○ warm
- ○ awful
- ○ pleasing

14 Find the sentence that best completes the story.

Beatrice watched Edward. _____. She tried to catch him.

- ○ She practiced speaking to him.
- ○ She ate chicken every day.
- ○ She wanted to have him for lunch.

15 Choose the word that belongs in the blank.

I don't like the way he keeps _____ at me.

- ○ stare
- ○ staring
- ○ stared

Directions: Here is a story about a sock. Read this story carefully. Then read each question. Darken the circle for the correct answer.

Irwin the Sock

by David J. Klein

My name is Irwin. I am a sock. I have had a long and exciting life.

I remember when Irma, my mate, and I were made. After we were made, we were squeezed into a box. The next light we saw was in a clothing store. Within an hour, Irma and I were bought by Mrs. Davidson.

Mrs. Davidson had gotten us for her son, Phil. Phil was a nice boy of ten. In the winter Phil stayed inside a lot. He practiced his violin. His feet were clean and his nails were neatly trimmed.

When spring arrived, soccer season began. Phil's feet got smelly. He pounded us as he ran and kicked. We did not like being worn for sports.

We got older. Phil wore us less and less. The last time I saw Irma was the day of a music contest. Phil was very nervous. He grabbed a thread on his other leg and began to pull and pull. Phil looked down to see what it came from. He realized that the thread on the floor was once his left sock. Irma never had a chance.

violin = something that makes music

Phil won the contest. He told his mother that we were his lucky socks. She could not throw me out.

Phil never wore me again. But if he has a soccer game or has to play his violin, he puts me in his pocket. I miss my dear Irma. But it's still exciting to be with Phil when his team wins a game or when he is on stage.

In a way, Irma's passing gave me a second chance, a new life.

16 What was the first thing that happened to Irwin and Irma after they were made?

○ They were worn by Phil when he played soccer.

○ They were worn by Phil when he played the violin.

○ They were sold.

○ They were put into a box.

17 Why didn't Irwin and Irma like soccer season?

○ They got smelly.

○ They did not like to play sports.

○ They had to go outside.

○ They got older.

18 Why did Phil pull Irma apart?

○ He thought she was lucky.

○ He was excited.

○ He was nervous.

○ He didn't like her.

19 Why does Phil put Irwin in his pocket?

- ○ He can't wear Irwin on his feet.
- ○ He thinks Irwin brings good luck.
- ○ He is afraid to rip Irwin.
- ○ He doesn't want his mother to throw Irwin out.

20 Which idea could not happen in real life?

- ○ In the winter Phil only stayed inside.
- ○ Irwin did not like being worn for sports.
- ○ Phil got nervous during music contests.
- ○ Irma fell apart.

21 How does Irwin feel at the end of the story?

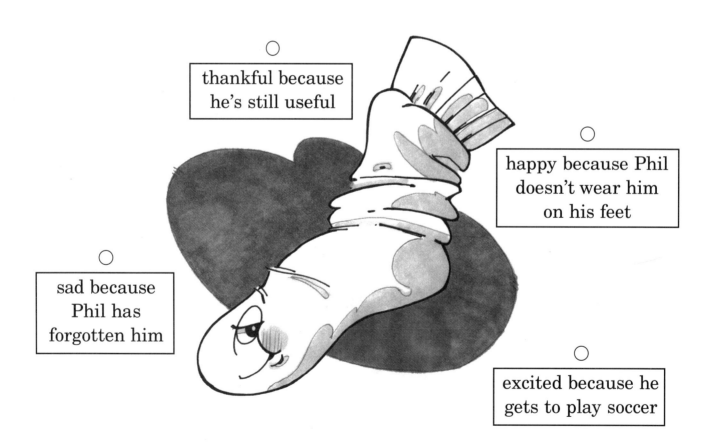

○ thankful because he's still useful

○ happy because Phil doesn't wear him on his feet

○ sad because Phil has forgotten him

○ excited because he gets to play soccer

22 **If you wanted to name a pair of your socks like Irwin and Irma were named, what could you call them?**

- ○ Andres and Anna
- ○ Bill and Silvia
- ○ Aaron and Erin
- ○ Daniel and Michelle

23 **Two matching socks are called a <u>pair</u>.**

What is something else that comes in a pair?

- ○ hats
- ○ jackets
- ○ gloves
- ◉ skirts

24 **Choose the word that belongs in the blank.**

Do you _____ socks every day?

- ○ wore
- ○ wear
- ○ wears
- ○ wearing

25 **Choose the word that belongs in the blank for <u>both</u> sentences.**

Turn off the _____ when you leave the room.

A box full of feathers is very _____.

- ○ radio
- ○ large
- ○ water
- ○ light

Directions: Here is a fairy tale. Read this story carefully. Then read each question. Darken the circle for the correct answer.

The Dragon of Worchester

by Jesse Lawrence

King John of Worchester was the richest king in all the land. Townsfolk often came to the castle asking for money. King John always refused.

The people began to get angry. More and more people started to come to the castle. As they did, King John began to worry. One morning more than fifty people came. "Remove them," King John told the guards. The people did not want to go. They gave the guards a hard time. Two people were put in the dungeon.

dungeon = underground jail

King John was worried. He knew more people would come the next day. That evening he set out to find help. He walked to a cave. "Dragon of Worchester," the king yelled inside. "I come to you in need."

King John heard a voice. "What is it, oh richest king?"

"I am worried about my people. I need someone to move them away. I can pay you a lot of money."

There was a long silence. Finally, the dragon spoke. "I will be there tomorrow as you have asked."

The next morning the king woke early to look for the dragon. He was nowhere to be found. By noon over one hundred people were gathered in front of the castle. They were all very angry.

"Coins for the people!" they yelled.

Then loud footsteps shook the ground. It was the dragon. King John ran to a window to speak to him. "I'm so glad to see you," he

told the dragon. "Do whatever is needed to rid me of these townsfolk."

townsfolk = people who live in a town

The dragon started to whack the castle with his tail. The side wall broke. Gold and silver came pouring out. The people heard the noise and rushed to see what it was. A large cheer went up as they grabbed the coins. After all the coins were gone, the people left.

"What have you done?" King John screamed to the dragon.

"I have helped you just as you asked. The people are gone." And with that, he disappeared.

26 Why did the townsfolk show up at the castle?

- ○ They were afraid of the dragon.
- ○ They were having a party.
- ○ They wanted to see King John.
- ○ They hoped to get money.

27 How would you describe King John?

- ○ selfish and cruel
- ○ rich and kind
- ○ happy and fair
- ○ brave and giving

28 Why did King John begin to worry?

- ○ He was afraid the townsfolk would hurt him.
- ○ He thought the townsfolk might hurt themselves.
- ○ He was in need of more money.
- ○ He felt his guards needed help.

29 How did the dragon get rid of the townsfolk?

- ○ He scared them away.
- ○ He took them to his secret cave.
- ○ He gave them what they wanted.
- ○ He tricked them.

30 How do you know that the dragon didn't like King John?

- ○ The dragon told King John he would not help him.
- ○ The dragon helped the townsfolk.
- ○ The dragon did not show up on time.
- ○ The dragon disappeared at the end.

31 This story teaches a lesson. What lesson does King John learn?

- ○ You should save your money.
- ○ You should be kind to others.
- ○ You should not trust dragons.
- ○ You should hide from danger.

32 Choose the sentence that is written correctly.

- ○ Them wanted money from King John.
- ○ The dragon helped his.
- ○ Those townsfolk were angry.
- ○ Her asked for some money.

33 Choose the word that belongs in the blank.

The dragon was _____ than King John.

- ○ nice
- ○ nicer
- ○ nicest
- ○ nicely

34 Choose the words that belong in the blank.

The king _____.

- ○ married to a queen
- ○ and his guards
- ○ worrying about the townsfolk
- ○ rules the country

35 Karla wrote this story about being a king. Choose the best topic sentence for the story.

_____. You must rule the people in your country. But you need to make them happy. You want them to like you.

- ○ Kings are rich people.
- ○ It must be fun to be king.
- ○ I don't know any kings.
- ○ It is hard to be a good king.

Directions: Here is a nursery rhyme. It is very old. Read this rhyme. Then read each question. Darken the circle for the correct answer.

OLD MOTHER HUBBARD

by Mother Goose

Old Mother Hubbard
   Went to the cupboard,
To give her poor dog a bone;
   But when she got there
The cupboard was bare,
   And so the poor dog had none.

She went to the baker's
   To buy him some bread;
When she came back
   The dog was dead.

She went to the undertaker's
   To buy him a coffin;
When she got back
   The dog was laughin'.

Directions: There are more verses to this nursery rhyme. Some of them are below. Choose the word or words that belong in the blanks.

She went to the __(36)__
    To buy him a hat;
When she came back
    He was feeding the cat.

She went to the barber's
    To buy him a __(37)__ ;
When she came back
    He was dancing a jig.

She went to the fruiterer's
    To buy him some fruit;
When she came __(38)__
    He was playing the flute.

She went to the cobbler's
    To buy him some shoes;
When she came back
    He was reading the __(39)__ .

36 ○ hatter's
    ○ pet store
    ○ undertaker's
    ○ cupboard

37 ○ shave
    ○ haircut
    ○ wig
    ○ hat

38 ○ home
    ○ mute
    ○ back
    ○ to her

39 ○ paper
    ○ lose
    ○ sack
    ○ news

STOP

Being the Best You Can Be

If you want to do well, first you have to try. Sometimes it is hard to do well. But you should always try to be the best you can be.

Now you will read about some people who have done great things. These people did not let anything stop them.

Directions: Here is a story about a baseball star. His name is Larry Doby. He was one of the first African-Americans to play in the major leagues. Read this story. Then read each question. Darken the circle for the correct answer.

One of Baseball's Best

At one time black and white baseball players could not play together. The major leagues were for white people. Black players had to play in the Negro league. That's the way it was until 1947. In that year Jackie Robinson and Larry Doby were the first African-Americans to play in the major leagues.

Larry was a home run hitter. He became one of the best players in the Negro league. In 1947 he hit more home runs than any other player. That was the year the owner of the Cleveland Indians asked Larry to play for them. Larry Doby joined the major leagues. Larry helped the Cleveland Indians win many games.

Fifty years later, in 1997, there were parties to celebrate what Larry Doby did. At one of the parties in Cleveland, 43,000 people stood up and cheered him. In 1998 Larry was picked for the Baseball Hall of Fame. Larry once said, "I wanted to play the best I could." Larry Doby was a great baseball player. He is also a great American.

league = a group of teams

Go

40 Why did the Cleveland Indians want Larry Doby to play for them?

○ because he was a great American

○ because he played all kinds of sports

○ because he was a home run hitter

○ because he was in the Negro league

41 How is Larry Doby like Jackie Robinson?

○ They loved to play basketball.

○ They were born in 1947.

○ They both helped the Cleveland Indians win many games.

○ They were the first African-Americans to play major league baseball.

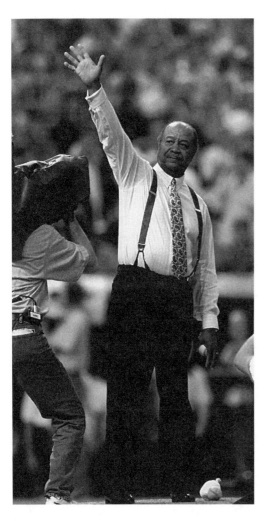

42 Why was Larry being honored in 1997?

○ He was one of the first black men to play major league baseball.

○ He had been elected into the Baseball Hall of Fame.

○ He was celebrating his birthday.

○ He had just helped the Cleveland Indians win a game.

43 Look at the photo of Larry Doby at the party in Cleveland. How do you think he felt?

○ happy because people remembered what he did

○ sad because many people had not heard of him

○ glad because he was playing baseball

○ angry because he could not play baseball

44 In 1997 there were parties to <u>celebrate</u> what Larry Doby did. Another word for <u>celebrate</u> is

- ○ tell
- ○ honor
- ○ refuse
- ○ show

45 A student wrote a story about Larry Doby. Choose the sentences that best complete the story.

Larry Doby was always a good ball player. As a child, he was the best player on his team. _____.

- ○ He played stickball in Camden, South Carolina. In high school he played all kinds of sports.
- ○ In 1948 the Cleveland Indians won the World Series. That was the last time they won.
- ○ He grew up to become a home run champ. He helped the Cleveland Indians win the World Series in 1948.
- ○ He played for the Kansas City Monarchs in the Negro league. He was paid $350.

46 Choose the sentence that is written correctly.

- ○ To hit the ball.
- ○ Playing the game of baseball.
- ○ He have not heard of Larry Doby.
- ○ You play stickball with a stick.

47 **Choose the sentence that best completes the story.**

> The World Series is played at the end of every baseball season.
> _____. The first team to win four games wins the series.

○ Opening day of the baseball season is in the spring.

○ The Cleveland Indians won the World Series in 1948.

○ The two top teams play each other.

○ People have been playing baseball since the 1800s.

48 **Choose the subject of the sentence.**

The <u>party</u> was a <u>surprise</u> for the <u>special</u> <u>guest</u>.

○   ○   ○ ○

49 **Choose the word that belongs in the blank.**

The Cleveland Indians were the _____ team in baseball in 1948.

○ good

○ better

○ best

○ bestest

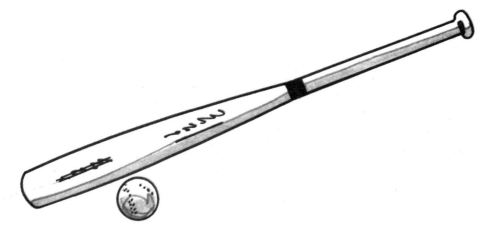

Directions: Choose the words with the correct capital letters and punctuation for the blanks.

June 16, 2002

(50)

I read about Larry Doby. He was an interesting man. I would like to send the book to you. I think you'll like it.

(51)

Ali

50 ○ dear jane
○ Dear jane
○ Dear Jane,

51 ○ Your cousin
○ Your cousin,
○ your cousin

Directions: Here is a student's report about Margaret Knight. The student made some mistakes. Read this story carefully. Then read each question. Darken the circle for the correct answer.

Margaret Knight — Young Inventor

[1.] Margaret Knight is my hero. [2.] She works in a cotton mill in the 1850s. [3.] A cotton mill were a place where they made cloth. [4.] Margaret's nickname was Matty. [5.] One day Matty saw someone get hurt. [6.] A girl was stuck by the sharp point of a machine. [7.] After that Matty inventing a new machine that was safer. [8.] Her was only 12 years old when she invented the machine. [9.] Matty invented about ninety more things during her life.

52 Choose the best way to write sentence 2.

○ She is working in a cotton mill in the 1850s.

○ She has worked in a cotton mill in the 1850s.

○ She worked in a cotton mill in the 1850s.

○ Best as it is.

53 Choose the best way to write sentence 3.

○ Cotton mills were a place where they made cloth.

○ A cotton mill was a place where they made cloth.

○ Cotton mills was a place where they made cloth.

○ Best as it is.

54 Choose the best way to write sentence 7.

○ After that Matty invented a new machine that was safer.

○ Matty inventing a new machine that was safer after that.

○ After that Matty has invented a new machine that was safer.

○ Best as it is.

55 Choose the best way to write sentence 8.

○ Her was only 12 years old when her invented the machine.

○ She was only 12 years old when she invented the machine.

○ She was only 12 years old when her invented the machine.

○ Best as it is.

Directions: Here is a story about a writer. Her name is Amy Tan. Read this story. Then read each question. Darken the circle for the correct answer.

Meet Amy Tan

When Amy Tan was a little girl, her family moved a lot. Amy missed her old friends. She wrote letters to these old friends. Amy did not want her letters to be boring. So she made up things to write about. That's how Amy learned to tell colorful tales. No wonder she grew up to be a book author.

Amy is an Asian-American. Her mother and father came from China. Amy was born and raised in California.

When she was young, Amy didn't like her nose. Amy did not want to look Chinese. Sometimes she wore a clothespin on her nose. Now Amy is proud to look Chinese. Her stories are about Chinese people who live in America.

Today her writing is famous. Her best known book is *The Joy Luck Club*. It is about four Chinese women who came to the United States. The book tells of how they raised their children in America.

56 Amy wrote made-up stories in her letters because

○ she was lonely

○ she did not want to bore her friends

○ she wanted to be an author when she grew up

○ she did not like her looks

57 Today Amy Tan's writing is <u>famous</u>.

Another word for <u>famous</u> is

○ forgotten

○ colorful

○ beautiful

○ well-known

58 Why did Amy probably write to her friends?

○ She wanted to stay friends with them.

○ She did not want to see them.

○ She had to practice her writing.

○ She was asked to write them by her parents.

59 Amy writes about growing up in America because

○ that is what she wrote in her letters

○ she does not know about China

○ that is the life she knows

○ she writes fairy tales

60 The story says Amy was "raised in California."

What does that mean?

○ She left California after she was born.

○ She liked living in California.

○ She grew up in California.

○ She moved to California.

Choose the words that belong in the blanks.

> I wish I were a writer like Amy Tan. I __(61)__ writing all the time.
> __(62)__ writing, I think of something funny that has happened to me.

61 ○ repeat   **62** ○ Before
     ○ learn   ○ After
     ○ read   ○ While
     ○ practice   ○ Under

63 Choose the sentence that best completes the story.

> When I was a little girl, I liked to read. _____. Now that I am older,
> I can buy my own books.

    ○ I go to the bookstore all the time.
    ○ My mother bought me all the books I loved.
    ○ I don't care to read anymore.
    ○ When I was a baby, my mother read to me.

64 **A student found out a lot about Amy Tan. She wrote a story about her. Choose the best topic sentence for her story.**

_____. She read a book a day when she was a kid. She loved fairy tales and the Laura Ingalls Wilder books.

○ Amy always loved to read.

○ Amy did very well in school.

○ Amy had a job writing speeches.

○ Amy remembers all of her teachers.

65 **Choose the sentence that has the correct capitalization and punctuation.**

○ Amy is asian-american.

○ Her Mother and Father came from China.

○ Amy was born in California

○ Today she lives in San Francisco.

66 **Choose the sentence that has the correct capitalization and punctuation.**

○ Amy Tan's mother became sick

○ Amy made a promise to her?

○ her mother got better.

○ They visited China together.

CHINA

67 Choose the sentence that is written correctly.

- ○ He have written many stories.
- ○ You can write on a computer.
- ○ Science fiction stories is the best.
- ○ I likes to write plays.

68 Choose the sentence that is written correctly.

- ○ Writing at night.
- ○ She loves reading.
- ○ Dreams to be told.
- ○ To be an author.

69 Choose the words that belong in the blank.

_____ wrote down her dreams.

- ○ The poet
- ○ Tomorrow afternoon
- ○ When the sun
- ○ Exciting and sad

70 Choose the sentences that best complete the story.

When I'm alone, I pretend I am a writer. _____.

- ○ I meet my friends. We all play together.
- ○ I go to the kitchen. There is always something to eat.
- ○ The dog comes into the house. He has muddy feet.
- ○ I sit at my desk and think. Then I write little stories.

Sample A

Mary has 6 uncles and 9 aunts. How many uncles and aunts does she have in all?

○ 13

○ 14

○ 15

○ 16

○ None of these

Sample B

Use the inch side of your ruler to solve this problem.

How many inches long is the pencil?

○ 7 inches

○ 6 inches

○ 5 inches

○ 4 inches

1 **4 x 9 =**

○ 13
○ 27
○ 36
○ 49
○ None of these

2 **78 – 5 =**

○ 73
○ 74
○ 28
○ 83
○ None of these

3 **48 ÷ 6 =**

○ 54
○ 42
○ 7
○ 9
○ None of these

4 **2.7 + 0.6 =**

○ 2.3
○ 2.76
○ 2.13
○ 3.3
○ None of these

5 **674**
  + 228

○ 802
○ 892
○ 902
○ 992
○ None of these

6 **559**
  – 523

○ 536
○ 26
○ 36
○ 63
○ None of these

7 **10**
  x 10

○ 100
○ 20
○ 1,000
○ 1,010
○ None of these

8 What number goes in the box to make the number sentence true?

$$6 + \square = 15$$

- ○ 21
- ○ 19
- ○ 11
- ○ 9

9 What number sentence tells how many brothers Kim and Tara have in all?

> Tara has five brothers.
> Kim has three brothers.

- ○ 5 + 3 = 2
- ○ 5 + 3 = 8
- ○ 5 − 3 = 2
- ○ 5 − 3 = 8

10 Hope bought two stamps. The total cost was 55 cents. She used a dollar. How much change did she get?

- ○ 55 cents
- ○ 45 cents
- ○ 35 cents
- ○ one dollar and 55 cents

11 Which number is the same as three thousand five hundred six?

- ○ 356
- ○ 3,560
- ○ 30,506
- ○ 3,506

12 What number is shown by the blocks in the picture below?

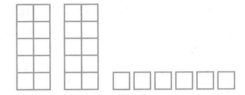

- ○ 206
- ○ 62
- ○ 26
- ○ 602

13 Which shape has exactly three sides?

- ○ triangle
- ○ square
- ○ rectangle
- ○ circle

Directions: Use estimation to find the best answers for problems 14 and 15.

14 Which number is closest to 213 + 480?

- ○ 500
- ○ 600
- ○ 700
- ○ 800

15 Suppose you pay for the two items below using a $20 bill. About how much change will you receive?

- ○ $11
- ○ $9
- ○ $8
- ○ $7

16 Look at the pattern below. What number comes next?

- ○ 35
- ○ 40
- ○ 55
- ○ 60

15, 20, 25, 30, ___

17 Daniel wrote numbers on the slips of paper shown below. He put them in a bag. He picks one slip of paper. What number will most likely show up?

- ○ 1
- ○ 2
- ○ 3
- ○ 4

18 Mike's Collectibles and Comics has this sign posted on its door.

MIKE'S
Hours
Monday — Friday
10AM — 5PM
Saturday
9AM — 4PM

Kiera wants to get to Mike's on Saturday as soon as it opens. It takes her 30 minutes to walk there from home. When should she leave her home?

○ 8:30 A.M.
○ 9:00 A.M.
○ 9:30 A.M.
○ 10:30 A.M.

19 What number goes in the box to make the number sentence true?

$$9 - \square = 3$$

○ 3
○ 6
○ 12
○ 27

20 There was a baseball game last night. There were 32,085 fans. Which number is in the thousands place of 32,085?

○ 3
○ 2
○ 0
○ 8

21 Which number in the box is greatest?

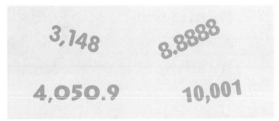

3,148   8.8888
4,050.9   10,001

○ 3,148
○ 10,001
○ 4,050.9
○ 8.8888

22 What shape appears next in the pattern?

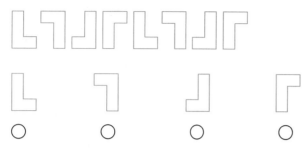

○   ○   ○   ○

23 The minute hand on a clock moved from the 3 to the 7. How many minutes passed?

○ 20 minutes
○ 15 minutes
○ 10 minutes
○ 4 minutes

24 Iris has more brothers than sisters. She has 10 brothers and sisters in all. How many sisters could she have?

○ 7
○ 6
○ 5
○ 4

25 What does the sign **not** tell you?

○ the price for a woman's haircut
○ the price for a boy's haircut
○ the time the store closes on Wednesday
○ the special price for kids under 3 years old

Caroline's Haircuts

Prices
Men and Women $12.00
Boys and Girls $8.00

Hours
Monday–Saturday
7am–7pm
Closed Sunday

26 Bonnie walked from the park to school. How could she walk?

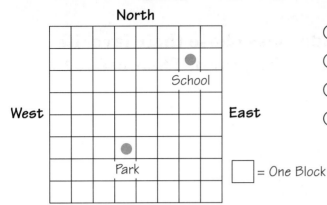

○ go 3 blocks west and 5 blocks south
○ go 4 blocks north and 3 blocks east
○ go 3 blocks east and 5 blocks north
○ go 5 blocks south and 3 blocks west

27 Use the inch side of your ruler. Which figure is 1 inch wide?

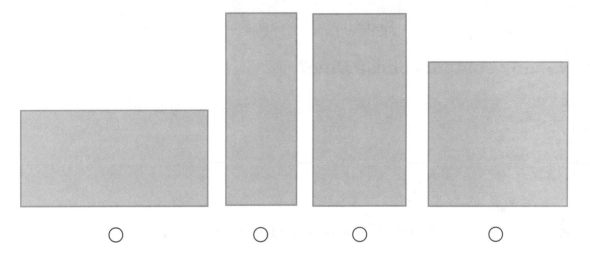

○   ○   ○   ○

28 Veronica wrote a capital letter V on a sheet of paper. She turned it upside down. It looked very different. Which letter looks the same when it is turned upside down?

○ capital letter F
○ capital letter G
○ capital letter H
○ capital letter J

OUR FAVORITE COLORS

Directions: The students in a third-grade class chose their favorite colors. The graph shows the results. Read the graph. Then use it to answer problems 29 through 31.

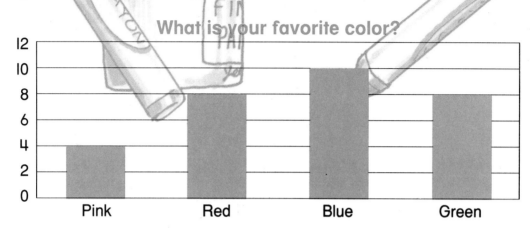

What is your favorite color?

	Pink	Red	Blue	Green

29 How many students chose Blue?

- ○ 10
- ○ 8
- ○ 5
- ○ 4

30 Which two colors were chosen by the same number of students?

- ○ Pink and Red
- ○ Red and Green
- ○ Red and Blue
- ○ Green and Blue

31 Two girls picked Red. How many boys picked Red?

- ○ 2
- ○ 4
- ○ 6
- ○ 8

32 Which shape is different from the rest?

○

○

○

○

33 Which fraction of the square is shaded?

○ $\frac{1}{3}$

○ $\frac{1}{4}$

○ $\frac{2}{3}$

○ $\frac{3}{4}$

34 August 1 was a Monday. What day of the week was August 31?

○ Monday

○ Wednesday

○ Friday

○ Sunday

35 What number is missing in the pattern?

8, 12, 16, ___, 24, ...

○ 17
○ 18
○ 19
○ 20

36 Which is most likely measured in pounds?

○ the height of a building
○ the depth of an ocean
○ the weight of a piano
○ the weight of a feather

37 Mr. Forbes made dinner last night. He cooked for his wife, himself, their six children, and four friends. How many dinners did Mr. Forbes make?

○ 10
○ 11
○ 12
○ 13

38 A calculator showed the number below. What number is one greater?

○ four thousand five hundred sixty
○ four thousand five hundred six
○ four thousand six hundred
○ four thousand six hundred sixty

39 A girl spins the spinner. Where will it most likely land after the spin?

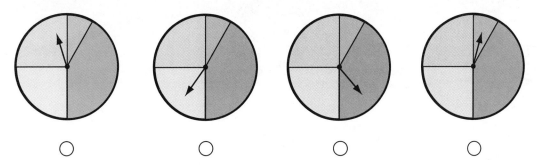

○   ○   ○   ○

40 Georgia has an odd number of dimes in her pocket. How much money could she have in dimes?

○ $1.00
○ $0.77
○ $0.60
○ $0.50

41 How many small triangles will there be in the next picture of the pattern?

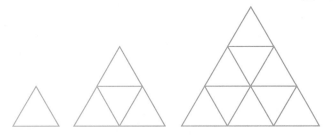

○ 16
○ 15
○ 14
○ 12

Which tool measures weight?

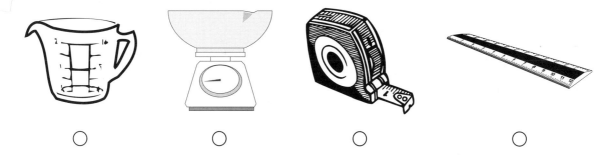

○   ○   ○   ○

43 **Ling is using these counters to solve a number sentence. Which number sentence could it be?**

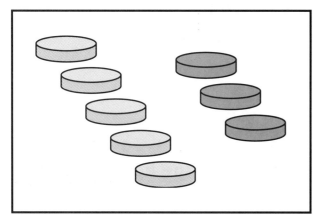

○ 5 x 3 = 15

○ 5 + 3 = 8

○ 5 − 3 = 2

○ 3 − 5 = 2

44 **Billy bought 1 comic book on Monday. He bought 2 comic books on Tuesday, and 3 comic books on Wednesday. Billy continues this pattern. How many comic books will he own by the end of Saturday?**

○ 6

○ 11

○ 15

○ 21

Directions: Riddel Beach School held sports sign-up day. Use the direction sign to answer problems 45 through 47.

45 What is the shape of the sign called?

○ rectangle

○ pentagon

○ hexagon

○ octagon

Sports Teams Sign-Up Day

Last Name begins with	Go to Room
A-F	107
G-M	121
N-S	214
T-Z	216

46 Andrea Punzalan wants to sign up for soccer. Where should she go?

○ Room 107

○ Room 121

○ Room 214

○ Room 216

47 Ninety students want to sign up for soccer. Sixty want to sign up for baseball. One-third of those students go to room 214. How many students is that?

○ 20

○ 30

○ 40

○ 50

SCHOOL ELECTIONS

Directions: Elections were held for third-grade president. The chart shows the results. Use the chart to answer problems 48 through 50.

Kiyo	卌 |
Darren	卌 卌
Robert	||||
Samantha	卌 卌 ||
Vishnu	卌 ||||

48 Who won the election?

○ Kiyo
○ Darren
○ Samantha
○ Vishnu

49 How many votes did Kiyo receive?

○ 11
○ 7
○ 6
○ 5

Vote for Kiyo

50 What is not on the chart?

○ how many students voted
○ who got the fewest number of votes
○ who came in second place
○ when the voting took place

Cut Out

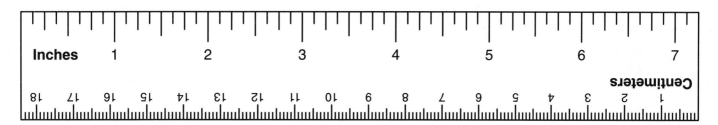